BILL ARP SO CALLED

A SIDE SHOW OF THE SOUTHERN SIDE OF THE WAR.

"I'M A GOOD UNION MAN 'SO CALLED' BUT I'LL BET ON DIXIE AS LONG AS I'VE GOT A DOLLAR."

ILLUSTRATED BY M. A. SULLIVAN

J. HOEY ENG.

METROPOLITAN RECORD OFFICE.
NEW YORK
1866.

BILL ARP,

SO CALLED.

A SIDE SHOW

OF THE

SOUTHERN SIDE OF THE WAR.

"I'm a good Union man, so-called; but I'll bet on Dixie as long as I've got a dollar."

ILLUSTRATED BY M. A. SULLIVAN.

NEW YORK:
METROPOLITAN RECORD OFFICE.
1866.

CONTENTS.

TO THE PUBLISHER.

Yours, requesting copies of my humorous letters for publication, is before me. I have thought that they were hardly worthy of being placed before the public in book form. At the time they were written they were appreciated, because the minds of the people needed relaxation from the momentous and absorbing interests of the war. The fountain of thought was tired, and these were its rest. The humor that is in them was entertaining then, for it was pertinent to the occasion that provoked it, and very impertinent to those it held up before the public eye.

I do not think that such humor will bear the wasting severity of time. It was once considered sparkling and exhilarating, but like good wine it has become stale from having been too long uncorked.

Nevertheless, these letters may be worthy of preservation, as illustrative of a part of the war—as a side-show to the Southern side of it—an index to our feelings and sentiments, and for this reason only I place them at your disposal. I must request, however, that in compiling them, you will thoroughly revise and reconstruct the orthography. When I began writing under the signature of Bill Arp, I was honestly idealizing the language and humor of an unlettered countryman who bears that name. I tried to write as he would, could he have written at all. His earnest, honest wit attracted my attention, and he declares to this day that I have faithfully expressed his sentiments. Those who know him can see more of him in my letters than they can of me, and in this view of my labors I may be suspected of playing Boswell to an uneducated and humorous man, whose name is not Johnson, but Arp.

Reflection has, however, convinced me that while good taste would not condemn one or two letters for murdering her Majesty's English, yet a frequent repetition of the offence can hardly be justified. It is demoralizing to language. The truth is, no wit is good wit that will not bear to be correctly written, and I therefore direct a reconstruction of the orthography, even at the peril of Mr. Arp's reputation.

For the sentiments that pervade these letters, I have no apology to make. At the time they appeared in the press of the South, these sentiments were the silent echoes of our people's thoughts, and this accounts in the main for the popularity with which they were received. Of course they contain exaggerations, and prophecies which were never fulfilled; but both sections were playing " brag " as well as " battle," and though we could not compete with our opponents in the former, yet some of us did try to hold our own. At both games we were whipped by overwhelming forces, and we have given it up. Conquered, but not convinced, we have accepted the situation, and have pledged ourselves to abide by it. We have sworn to do so. We have declared it most solemnly in convention. We have asserted it in every act and deed; and Southern honor, which our enemies cannot appreciate, but which is untarnished and imperishable, is the seal of our good faith. Whoever testifies to the existence among us of an association designing a renewal of the rebellion, is either the victim of his own cowardice, or else the author of a selfish and heartless lie. I say this with feeling and indignation, for we see in such testimony a willingness, nay, a desire on the part of our military rulers, to retain over us their power and their tyranny for malicious or avaricious ends. We have long felt, and we still are feeling, their insults, their black mail, their robberies. Ours is the stranded ship, and the Federal officers among us are the wreckers; ours the carcass, and they the vultures who are picking our denuded bones. The little that was left our people is seized, and released on paying a part into private pockets. They get rich and resign, and a fresh corps of vampires take their places, to renew the operation. I have even known them to steal by night, and haul away the poor pittance of damaged corn that our generous (?) Government had stored for distribution to our starving poor. It is for such purposes that military dominion is to be continued. Would that this were all! But not content with even this exhaustion of our scanty means, they are annulling our contracts made with the laborers who were content to work in our fields for fair wages, and are tolling them off to parts unknown under false pretences. Our ploughs are standing in the fields idle, our farms will go untilled, and the land swarms with agents who are bribing the poor negroes away under promises of higher wages, and under the sanction of a Bureau as rotten as the promises of Pharoah.

Væ victis. But still we abide all these sad results, and look upon it as part of the war, and in keeping with the character of those who have so long been our enemies. They but exhibit the animus of a people whose hate and avarice induced the rebellion. Such oppression has turned from them almost the last opponent of secession, and caused them to regret that they did not throw their lives and fortunes into the fight.

Perhaps this is all for the best. We cannot tell. We have almost ceased to philosophize upon it, for we have no time to think. The work of actual reconstruction absorbs our time and energies. I mean the reconstruction of our individual fortunes, our houses, our fields and farms, our railroads, manufactures, graveyards, schools, and churches. We have no time to stop and mourn over the loss of liberty.

But I can find time to ask, What has the North gained by the war? What principles have been established? What great or vital questions have been settled? Is the sovereignity of a State forever annulled? Then let Illinois take down her deceitful sign, obliterate her great seal of State, and choose another, for the one she now has is obsolete—*an eagle proudly postured under a scroll, with "State sovereignty"* upon it. Is it the freedom of slaves that has been accomplished? Alas! the one and a half millions who have perished in the war, are certainly free; the remainder are rapidly realizing the same liberty, or finding a new bondage in other climes. Like the poor Indian, the race is doomed, and the mighty North still triumphs in the glory of its accomplishment. But I will not speak more of this. To the charitable reader let me say, Forgive me if you find something to condemn in the following pages. It is not in my heart to offend a good man, whether he live North or South; and there be better judges than I of what should have, or have not been written. It may be said that the character of these letters has no tendency to soften the animosities engendered by the late unhappy strife. I can only answer, that it is not in rebel nature to be humble to those who would put the heel of tyranny upon us. Our people are a unit upon the moral of the fight they made. They sincerely feel that the provocation of the war was not of their begetting. Many a time and oft have men and nations been conquered, but not convinced. The story of Ireland, Poland, and the "Hero of the Lakes," has been often reproduced, to illustrate that wrongs are not remedied, nor rights secured, by wager of battle. John Huss suffered martyrdom for that which Luther accomplished a century later.

While mourning the loss of thousands of the noblest of our race, while suffering the poverty and desolation with which our conquerors have visited us, while memory stings with the rape and arson which barbarians under arms enforced and heartless officers permitted, it is not in human nature to smother resentment against those who would still play the tyrant and grind us into dust.

But to you, kind reader, who can speak gently to

the erring (if we have erred), who would pour oil upon the troubled waters, and prefer the hand of kindred love, let me say that, though proudly defiant of our enemies, the noble manliness of our peeple will meet you cordially at the first sincere effort toward an honorable reconciliation. Otherwise we will close up the avenues of our hearts, and, like the red man of the forest, transmit our bitterness and our wrongs as a heritage to our children.

Republicans, Puritans, Pharisees, Saints--you who were suckled with songs of pity for the charcoal race, whose hypocritical sympathies have been for years playing leap-frog over the poverty and distress around your own doors, and alighting far off in the sunny land; who have seen and are seeing thousands of your dusky pets perishing and passing away, from the lack of food and the lust of freedom; you whose morning hymn is, "I love my love with a B, because he is black," and whose evening prayer, "May the Lord send freedom, without money and without price;" you who look upon our people as a race of turbulent devils, and a foul blot upon the good name of the land--to you I commend all the comfort that you can find within these pages. Small though this volume be, it will nevertheless save you the exclaiming, "Oh that mine adversary had written a book!"

CHARLES H. SMITH.

In regard to the request of the distinguished author, as to the reconstruction of the orthography, we have only to say that we have done our best; but if we have not always succeeded, it must be attributed to the rebellious character of the language. We have tried hard to make it "harmonize" with the strict rules laid down by Messrs. Murray and Webster, and trust we shall be acquitted from any complicity in the design against "Her Majesty's English," if in some instances the "spell" has not been altogether broken.

EDITOR OF THE METROPOLITAN RECORD.

NOTE.—Four letters of the series appeared first in the "Record," for which the author still continues at intervals to write.

BILL ARP IN HIS SANCTUM.

BILL ARP.

A CARD.

THE suffering Public are notified that I have opened an office at No. 2 Broad Street, with the professed object of establishing a business, very novel in its nature, but the necessity of which has long been felt in this community, and never so much so as at this time.

I propose to keep continual and unremitting watch upon the street, and in the counting-rooms, and lawyers' offices, and elsewhere, and bring immediate relief to any person, or set of persons, who may be held in "durance vile," or in any way be imposed upon by one of that class commonly called the "Bores of Society." By the aid of calculus and other high branches of mathematics, I have made an actual calculation of the number of hours lost by business men in this community, by reason of having to show unwilling attention to unwelcome visitors, and I find a clear loss (at ten cents an hour) of $6,732.49 per annum—which amount I will undertake for a reasonable compensation to save.

I suppose it is unnecessary for me to enlarge in this prospectus upon the provoking annoyance of being compelled, through courtesy, to *endure a man*, when your business or your pleasure makes you wish him a thousand miles away—which annoyance, if estimated in dollars and cents, would double the aforementioned sum.

I therefore proceed to show how I will release the sufferer without giving offence. I have prepared a system of signs, winks, and blinks, which I communicate in confidence to my patrons, and when I perceive one of them detained on the street or elsewhere by a Bore, I will *time* the interview, and after five minutes will call to him myself, or have one of our society to do so, and say, "I wish to see him on important business as soon as he gets through;" of course the sufferer can then have an excuse to bring the conversation to a sudden close. If the "Bore" is reading to him a long political letter, or a speech in some newspaper, or giving a history of how they did things where he was raised, or is rehearsing a long story preparatory to asking a loan of money, or security, or a little office, or some official influence, I will manage to catch his eye, and if he gives me the sign, or the wink or the blink, I will have him called off abruptly. If a dull preacher shall more than three times inflict a sermon of an hour and a half upon his congregation, I will, at the fourth time, very certainly cut off the last half hour by having one of my trained subordinates to cry "*Fire*" in the neighborhood of the church.

Should the doctors of this city come into my plan, I will save them the useless expenditure of paying confidential negroes to call them out of church during service, under pretence that they are professionally wanted. I will have them called out myself in such a *hasty* manner as to attract very general attention.

I shall keep a register of all the Bores of the county—classifying them as class No. 1—or Bores "*per se.*" This class are Bores everywhere and anywhere, and for them there is no hope of reform. Class No. 2—or Bores "*Occasional.*" This class are capable of good behavior, and sometimes, though seldom, are guilty of it. Class No. 3—or Bores "*Standant.*" This class are of a restless nature, and will stop you on the street and *stand* it out with you. They can bore twenty men in a day without wearying the big muscle in the calf of the leg. Class No. 4—or Bores "*Sittant.*" This is the most disagreeable and the most numerous class. They are fond of fire in the winter and shade in the summer, and will sit, and set, and sot, till your chair-bottoms will sink into the shape of an oyster-shell. I shall furnish each of my patrons with a list of these Bores. But the most important of my duties will be to relieve debtors from the importunity of their creditors. There are various modes of dunning, varying between the two extremes of the genteel and the disgusting. There is a class who will sit, and wait, and hang about you like a nightmare, when perhaps you are busy with a client or a customer, or talking to a friend—who manages to call on you at the most disagreeable time—who will carry his bill in his left-side pocket, with your name and the dollars and cents exposed on the outside of the bill—who can meet you at more corners and crossings, and whose shadow you can never escape—who will sit by your fire, and even put on more wood, to show that he came to besiege you till he got money or blood—who, when told you have no funds, wants to know *when you will have some*, and continues his inquiries to your utter disgust—who is wholly unable to distinguish a sensitive man from one of hard slate. Such Bores I style Bores "G.," which stands for *Gallinippers*, and my plan is, when one of my patrons is so bedevilled, I will call upon the sufferer and dun him *myself*, *gently*, for a dollar or so; and if he tells me he has no change, I will apologize in courteous language and manner for disturbing him, and will remark, "that I will wait *his* convenience hereafter, for I know he will pay when he has the means." I will retire, and if the Bore does not do so too in five minutes, I will return and seize him by the nap of the neck, and kick him out of doors. For this conduct I will hold myself personally responsible (having already fought my way from Northern Europe to this place); but if the grand jury should make any memorandum of the affair, I shall expect some four or five of my patrons to be near the court-house at Trial term, so that they may *accidentally* be caught on the jury. To accomplish this the more easily, I shall take the clerk, sheriffs, and judge into my society free of charge.

The above is the general programme. For the details and for admission, apply to

Dr. HELLE BORE,
No. 2 Broad Street.

BILL ARP TO ABE LINCOLN.

Rome, Geo., *April*, 1861.

Mr. Lincoln—

Sir: These are to inform you that we are all well, and hope these lines may find you in *statu quo.* We received your proclamation, and as you have put us on very short notice, a few of us boys have concluded to write you, and ask for a little more time. The fact is, we are most obliged to have a few more days, for the way things are happening, it is utterly impossible for us to disperse in twenty days. Old Virginia, and Tennessee, and North Carolina are continually aggravating us into tumults and carousments, and a body can't disperse until you put a stop to such unruly conduct on their part. I tried my darn'dst yesterday to disperse and retire, but it was no go; and besides, your marshal here ain't doing a darn'd thing—he don't read the riot-act, nor remonstrate, nor nothing, and ought to be turned out. If you conclude to do so, I am authorized to recommend to you Colonel Gibbons or Mr. McClung, who would attend to the business as well as most anybody.

The fact is, the boys around here want watching, or they'll take something. A few days ago I heard they surrounded two of our best citizens because they were named Fort and Sumter. Most of them are so hot that they fairly siz when you pour water on them, and that's the way they make up their military companies here now —when a man applies to join the volunteers, they sprinkle him, and if he sizzes they take him, and if he don't they don't.

Mr. Lincoln, sir, privately speaking, I'm afraid I'll get in a tight place here among these bloods, and have to slope out of it, and I would like much to have your Scotch cap and cloak that you travelled in to Washington. I suppose you wouldn't be likely to use the same disguise again when you left, and therefore I would propose to swap. I am five feet five, and could get my plough breeches and coat to you in eight or ten days if you can wait that long. I want you to write to me immediately about things generally, and let us know where you intend to do your fighting. Your proclamation says something about taking possession of all the private property at "All Hazards." We can't find no such a place on the map. I thought it must be about Charleston, or Savannah, or Harper's Ferry, but they say it ain't anywhere down South. One man said it was a little factory on an island in Lake Champlain, where they make sand-bags. My opinion is, that sand-bag business won't pay, and it is a great waste of money. Our boys here carry their sand in their gizzards, where it keeps better, and is always handy. I'm afraid your Government is giving you and your Kangaroo a great deal of unnecessary trouble, and my humble advice is, if things don't work better soon, you'd better grease it, or trade the darn'd old thing off. I'd take rails or any thing for it. If I could see you, I'd show you a sleight-of-hand trick that would change the whole concern into buttons quick. If you don't trade or do something else with it soon, it will spoil or die on your hands certain.

Give my respects to Bill Seward and the other members of the Kangaroo. What's Hannibal doing? I don't hear any thing from him now-a-days.

Yours, with care,

BILL ARP.

P. S.—If you can possibly extend that order to thirty days, do so. We have sent you a CHECK at Harper's Ferry (who keeps that darn'd old Ferry now? it's giving us a heap of trouble), but if you positively won't extend, we'll send you a check, drawn by Jeff. Davis, Beauregard endorser, payable on sight anywhere. Yours,

B. A.

TO MR. ABE LINCOLN.

CENTREVILLE, *January* 12, 1862.

MR. LINCOLN—

SIR: In the spring of the year I wrote you a letter from my native soil, asking for a little more time to disperse. I told you then that twenty days were not enough—that the thing could not be done in that brief interval. You can look back and see I was right. We tried our durndest to comply with your schedule, but as you kept calling for volunteers, our Cherokee Georgia Democrats kept coming out from under their clay roots. They shook themselves and spit fire, and wouldn't go back so long as the Whigs would read them the news about this fuss.

Mr. Abe Lincoln, sir, the spring has shed its fragrance, the summer is over and gone, the yellow leaves of autumn have covered the ground, old Winter is slobbering his froth on the earth, but we have not been able to disperse as yet. Me and the boys started last May to see you personally, and ask for an extension of your brief furlough, but we got on a bust in old Virginia, about the 21st of July, and like to have got run over by a parcel of fellows running from Bull Run to your city. After that we tried to get to you by the Potomac River, but Mr. Whiting said you were not running that machine *at these presents.* We next went to Mr. Harper's Ferry, to take the Baltimore Railroad, but we couldn't find the conductor, and cars seemed scarce, and the folks said you were not running that machine *much.* We thought, however, to take a deck passage on the canal, but a dam had broke and General Jackson said you were not running that machine, *scarcely any.* After all that we came back, and thought we'd get Captain Wilkes to ship us over, but Mr. Bennett sent us word that the captain had quit a seafaring life. Mr. Seward made him quit, to pacify an old English Bull that was bellowing about and pawing dirt in the air. Mr. Lincoln, sir, if that Bull is of the same stock as the one your folks saw here in July, he is dangerous, and will have a bad effect on your population. You had better circumscribe him before he hurts somebody.

Mr. Lincoln, sir, what are your factories doing now-a-days? I heard you had quit running their machines, owing to a thin crop of cotton. If you would put sweet oil on your factories, they wouldn't rust while standing idle. I was glad to hear that you had got enough cotton to do yours and Seward's families. The boys say you got enough to make as many shirts as Falstaff had in his company.

Mr. Lincoln, sir, how do you come on with your stone fleet—does it pay expenses—is it a safe investment—could

I get any stock in it at a fair price? Don't you think it is most too far to haul rocks, and won't it impoverish New England soil to take the rocks off of it?

Mr. Abe Lincoln, sir, the 18th is the anniversary of the day when Georgia tore herself frantically loose from the abolition dynasty—when she ripped her star from off the striped rag, and spread a new shirting to the breeze. We calculate to celebrate that day, and I am authorized to invite you and Bill Seward over to partake of our hospitalities. Where is Hamlin? I allow that he is dead, or I would ask him too. Let me know if you and Seward are coming, so we can fix up and swap a lie or two with you. Couldn't you all come along with Mack when he makes that advance he has been talking about so long? Bring your knitting with you when you come, and a clean shirt or two. Do you chaw tobacco? We have got some that is good. Ely chawed, and Mr. Davis gave him a whole warehouse at Richmond.

Mr. Lincoln, sir, I wish you would ask Banks to send me a codfish. Pole-cats are bad around here, and we want something to drive 'em away. If you bring Banks and Picayune Butler with you, you needn't bring the cod.

Yours, till death,

BILL ARP.

P. S.—Where is Fremont? I hear he has gone up a spout.

ANOTHER LETTER FROM BILL ARP TO MR. LINCOLN.

December 2, 1862.

MR. LINCOLN—

SIR: A poet has said that "Time untied waiteth for no man." To my opinion it is untied now and hastens on to that eventful period which you have fixed when Africa is to be unshackled, when Niggerdom is to feel the power of your proclamation, when Uncle Tom is to change his base and evacuate his cabin, when all the emblems of darkness are to rush frantically forth into the arms of their deliverers, and with perfumed and scented gratitude embrace your Excellency and Madam Harriet Beecher Stowe! What a glorious day that is to be! What a sublime era in history! What a proud culmination and consummation and corruscation of your political hopes! After a few thousand have clasped you in their ebony arms it will be a fitting time, Mr. Lincoln, for you to lay yourself down and die. Human ambition can have no higher monument to climb. After such a work you might complete the immortal heroism of your character, by leaping from the topmost pinnacle of your glory upon the earth below.

But alas for human folly—alas for all sublunary things—our people will not believe, these crazy rebels will not consider; Christmas is already here, only one more brief week to slide away before we must part, forever part, with all our negro heritage, and yet our stubborn people continue to buy and sell them, and the shorter the lease, the higher the price they are paying. What infatuation! I do verily believe they will keep up their old ways until next Wednesday night, just as though they did not have to give them all up the next morning before breakfast. Some say the stay law affects the niggers and will operate to make them stay at home—some say you have not got transportation nor rations for four millions of darkeys—some say your call is premature; but the majority are of the opinion that a little difficulty you met at Fredericksburg has interfered with your arrangements, and extended the time like a sine die.

Mr. Lincoln, sir, I forewarned you about crossing those sickly rivers. The Lee side of any shore is unhealthy to your population; keep away from those Virginia water-courses, go around them or under them, but for the sake of economy don't try to cross them. It is too hard upon your burial squads and ambulance horses.

Mr. Lincoln, sir, when is this war to close? How much longer can you renew your note of ninety days which you said was time enough to settle this difficulty—do you pay the interest? How much territory have you subjugated—what makes cotton sell at 67 cents a pound in your diggins—is it not awful scarce—what do your bony women do for stuffing and padding? I heard they had to use hay and saw-dust and such like, and I thought it must be very painful to their tender bosoms to have to resort to such scarce commodity; I would like to send you a bale, but Governor Brown would seize it. It is said by many that the war is about to close because of the Governor's late raid on leather—they say the war begun with a John Brown raid in Virginia, and will end with a Joe Brown raid in Georgia—I allow not, for I think the Governor only took that way of getting the State rid of its surplus, for he wanted to drive it into the adjoining States where things were scarcer. I would like to see you personally, Mr. Lincoln, and hear you talk and tell some of your funny anecdotes, like you told Governor Morehead. I laughed when I read them till the tears fairly rained from my eyelids—I know I could make my fortune, Mr. Lincoln, compiling your wit. May I be your Boswell, and follow you about?

But fare thee well, my friend, and, before you cross another Rubicon, I advise you, in the eloquent language of Mr. Burke, "consider, old cow, consider."

Yours, till death,

BILL ARP.

P. S.—Give my respects to Johnny Van Buren; I heard you and him were mighty thick and affectionate.

B. A.

ANOTHER LETTER FROM BILL ARP TO MR. LINCOLN.

Mr. Lincoln—

Sir: Is it not possible that you are using too much proclamation? More than eighteen months ago you published an edict, ordering the boys to retire and be peaceable, but they disretired and went to fighting. The effect was bad, very bad. Now you have proclaimed the negroes free after January, and I am afraid it will prove a fee-simple title for all time.

Every free negro will get in the cotton-patch now, sure; for the tarnal rebels do every thing by contraries. Negroes have risen twenty per cent., and are growing darker and blacker every day. A big plantation now looks like the sun was in an eclipse. Your proclamation has entailed Africa upon us so strong that you can actually smell it. Tippio says (we call him Tip for short) that he is personally interested, and he thinks you had better make them free first and issue your proclamation afterwards. General Hunter tried it your way, and over-cropped himself. Tip got no free papers at all.

Mr. Lincoln, sir, I am afraid you are taking in more ground than you can tend. You are trying to do too much at once. General Hunter tried your plan and couldn't work it over three States, so you had better practise on homœopathic doses. If you will begin on Dade County you can tell what your machine will do, as there is but one nigger there, and they keep him in a cage as a curiosity. If they will not accept your freedom, why, let them alone. It is useless to call them if they won't come. I once heard a fellow in a theatre say he could call spirits from the nasty deep, but the spirits never come and he got nary drink—so go it gently, Mr. Lincoln, but go it sure. The world, the flesh, and the devil are looking to you to extend the ægis of freedom over all creation—over things animate and inanimate—over bull bats and screech-owls, grub-worms and grindstones, niggers and alligators, and every thing that don't spill as the earth turns upside down. You will have a free fight, Mr. Lincoln, in doing all this, but never mind—pitch in—great is your reward.

Mr. Lincoln, sir, it is amazing to think what a big job you have undertaken. It is a big job, sure. Matthy Mattics nor his daddy couldn't figure out how long it will take you to get through according to your feeble progress. The double rule of three won't touch it, nor tare and tret. Great Bethel! what a power of work! Had you not better sublet the contract to some European nations? Sure as you are born you will need a heap of *undertakers* before you finish your overland march. If you could march like Jackson it would do, but you can't. Dr. Battey says that Jackson's troops take the gout if they rest twenty-four hours.

Mr. Lincoln, sir, our people get more stubborn every day. They go mighty near naked, and say they are saving their Sunday clothes to wear after we have whipped you. They just glory in living on half rations, and stewing salt out of their smoke-house dirt. They say they had rather fight you than feed you, and swear by the ghost of Calhoun they will eat roots and drink branch-water the balance of time before they will kernowly to your abolition dynasty. Chickahominy! what a job you have undertaken! Does Hannibal help you any? I hear tell that he just set in the corner of your office all day long, and never said a word but *nigger*, *nigger*, *nigger*, and that since your proclamation his face has turned darker and his hair more kinky.

Mr. Lincoln, sir, have you any late news from Mr. Harper's Ferry? I heard that Stone W. Jackson kept the parole for a few days, and that about fourteen thousand crossed over in twenty-four hours. He is a smart ferryman, sure. Do your folks know how to make it pay? It is a bad crossing, but I suppose it is a heap safer than Ball's Bluff or Sheppardstown. These are dangerous fords, Mr. Lincoln, sure, and I am afraid if your folks keep crossing such sickly rivers as the Potomac and Chickahominy, you will have all the scum of your population killed up, and you will have to encroach on your good society.

Mr. Lincoln, sir, your generals don't travel the right road to Richmond nohow. The way they have been trying to come is through a mighty Longstreet, over two powerful Hills, and across a tremendous Stonewall. It would be safer and cheaper for 'em to go around by the Rocky Mountains, if spending time in military excursions is their chief object.

But I must close this brief epistle. I feel very gloomy, Mr. Lincoln, about this destructive war, and have no heart to write much. As General Byron said, "I ain't now what I used to was, and my spirits are fluttering, faint, and low."

Yours, till death,

BILL ARP.

P. S.—How is Bill Seward? I heard that a mad dog bit him the other day, and the dog died immediately. Is it a fact?

B. A.

BILL ARP ON EXTORTIONERS.

Mr. Editor:

I have of late been home to the sunny South, where I reasonably expected the embraces of my friends and the civilities of numerous acquaintances. I did not assume the usual airs of a returned soldier, but was the same humble individual I was before the war and the mumps and measles broke out. I conversed generally about the boys and the sutlers, and the Tiger Rifles, and did not allude on no occasion to my intimacy with General Johnston and Toombs and such like.

The Home Guard frequently asked me why General Johnston did not fight more and retreat less, and when was I going back, and what so many came home for. I considered some of their questions very impertinent. The Guard are the talking part of a smart army, who are going to the war when it becomes actually necessary. From their casual remarks, I inferred they looked on us boys in the service as the pickets and outposts, while they themselves were the grand Bonaparte Reserve that were chafing and chewing their bits, and getting ready to *flank something.*

For an occupation, most of them have engaged in the extortion business of one sort or another—playing *home sutler* to the soldiers' wives and children. They *flanked* me in double quick, and though my time was not out, I was constrained to depart those coasts prematurely for fear of being a desolated victim of extortion. I suffered most pitiful in every contact. Having undertook to recruit my family supplies, my pocket book looked like an elephant had trod on it before I was half through. It took three months' pay to buy a pair of shoes and a fine-tooth comb. Shoeing and shirting and hatting the children was indefinitely postponed, and I quit those regions, leaving my wife wearing my old boots, and my boys dropping corn for an extortioner at three cents an acre. Jake said *he* was a little *rebel* and wouldn't do it; the last I saw of him he was digging bait. I say it with pride and satisfaction that my wife is an industrious and managing woman. She said she could squeeze out a living until blackberries come, if they come early, and then she was safe for a month longer. If any woman can she can, but it will be nip and tuck.

The rolling wheels of time and the cars brought me once more to the city of Richmond, where I stopped awhile to look around and feel of the public pulse. Calculating on being elected captain of my company at the reorganization, I thought I would look at a uniform. I called at the big store, and priced a set, and was asked one hundred and ninety-two dollars for coat and breeches;

whereupon I retired. Finding I could do no better, I went back next day to leave my dimensions, but found they had riz to *two hundred.* I retired again and went *straight to my camp.* It all turned out right, for when the time come, I wasn't elected, and I am still shedding out my patriotism at eleven dollars a month. There is not much margin for extortion on the Government at that price, I reckon.

It seems utterly impossible to get the extortioners in the ranks. Governor Brown thought he would put some of 'em to the useful art of bullet-stopping, so he called for a draft. Enough of the patriotic responded, and there was no draft. But it give 'em a powerful scare, and developed more rheumatics and chronics than was thought possible to exist in a limestone country. The doctors had oceans of fun examining the candidates for invalid honors. Well, after the fourth of March, they generally recovered and went to extortioning again, and continued until Congress passed the Conscript Bill, when they collapsed immediately, and all the invisible diseases returned. The doctors are, however, refusing to give 'em certificates, and the fun is equal to a circus. They are now bidding high on substitutes, and will get 'em, so I don't see much chance to stop these vampires from pursuing their occupation. If they could all be got in one regiment and put in the front ranks, with old Stonewall behind 'em, so they couldn't *renig*, wouldn't old rheumatics and chronics and two per cent. sing " farewell, vain world."

2*

But they will catch it in the long run. A spiritual medium in our camp, says as how old Lucifer is preparing a factory to make double distilled torment for traitors and extortioners. He has got his apparatus and chemicals all ready, and is only waiting for the carcasses of a few more, to use in his furnaces in place of soap-stone. He now has a side show of Vampires, and Hyenas, and Gorillas, to suck 'em, and gnaw 'em, and chaw 'em. This torment manufactory for extortioners and traitors is no romantic idea. More than a century ago, an eloquent and prophetic poet wrote—

"Is there not some secret curse, red with immortal wrath,
Some frenzied anguish, some Vesuvian fire,
Some torment thrice distilled, seething for him
Who builds his greatness on his country's ruin?"

I think so—of course. Farewell for the present,

Yours truly,

BILL ARP.

BATTLE OF ROME—OFFICIAL.

ROME, GA., *May*, 1863.

MESSRS. ADAIR & SMITH :

So many unreliable persons will be circulating spurious accounts of the "Grand rounds" took by the infernal Yankees in these ROMEantic regions, that I think it highly proper you should git the strait of it from one who seen it with his eyes, and heard it with his years, and a piece of it fell on his big toe.

More than two hundred years ago, General D. Soto had a big fight with the Indians on or about these consecrated grounds. Since that time an uninterrupted peace has rained around these classic hills and hollows. Flowers have bloomed sweetly, lambs have skipped about, dog fennel has yallered the ground, and the Coosa River, which was then but a little spring branch, has grown both wide and deep, until now the majestic steamboat can float upon its bosom, and the big mud cat gobble up the earth worms that chance to fall into its waters.

But rolling years will change a programme! Anno domini will tell. Just before the break of day on Sunday the third of May, 1863, the citizens of the Eternal City were aroused from their slumbers with the chorus of the Marseilles hymn. "To arms, to arms ye brave; Abe Lincoln is pegging away; the Yankees are riding to Rome on a raid." Ah! then was the time to try men's souls; but there was no panic, no skedaddling, no shaking of knees; but one universal determination to do something. The burial squad organized first and foremost, and began to inter their money, and spoons, and four-pronged forks, and such like, in small graves about the premises. Babies were sent to the rear. Horses hid in the cane-brake. Cows milked uncommonly dry. Cashiers and bank agents carried off their funds in a pair of saddle bags, which very much exposed their facilities and the small compass of their resources. It was, however, a satisfactory solution of their refusing to discount for the last three months. Scouts were sent out on every road to snuff the tainted breeze. Cotton bags were piled up across every high way and low way. Shot guns and cannon, powder and ball, were brought to the front. The yeomanry and the militia joined a squad of Confederate troops, and formed in line of battle. They were marched across the Oostanaula River, and then the plank of the bridge torn up so that they couldn't retreat. This was done, however, at their own valiant request, because of the natural weakness of the flesh. They determined jointly and severally firmly by these presents to *do something.*

CAMANCHE COURIER. p. 37.

Two cracked cannon, that had holes in the ends, and two or three in the sides, were propped up between the cotton bags, and pointed strait down the road to Alabama. They were first loaded with buckshot and tacks, and then a round ball rammed on top. The ball was to take the raid in the front, and the bullets and tacks to rake 'em in the flank. These latter it was supposed would go through the cracks in the side, and shoot around generally. Everybody and every thing determined to die in their tracks or *do something.* The steamboats dropped quietly down the river, to get out of the thick of the fight. The sharpshooters got on top of cemetery hill with their repeaters and pocket pistols. The videttes dashed with their spy glasses to the top of the court-house to see afar off. Dashing Camancha couriers rode unruly steeds to and fro like a fiddler's elbow. Some went forward to reconnoitre as scouts; first in the road and then out of the road; some mounted, and some on foot. All were resolved to *do something.*

At this critical juncture, and previous and afterwards, reports were brought into these headquarters, and all other quarters, to the effect that 10,000 Yankees were coming, and 5,000, and 2,000, and any other number; that they were ten miles from town, and six miles, and two miles, and any other number of miles; that they were on the Alabama road, and the Cave Spring road, and the river road, and any other road; that they were crossing the river at Quinn's ferry, and Williamson's ferry, and Bell's ferry, and any other ferry; that they had taken the steamboat "Laura Moore," and "Cherokee," and "Alfaratta," and any other steamboat; that they had shot a Camancha courier, and had hit him in the coat tail, or his horse's tail, or any other tail; that they had seized Cis Morris, Bill Morris, or Jep Morris, or any other Morris. In fact, a man could hear any thing by going about, and more too.

Sure enough, however, the important crisis which was to have arrived did actually arrive, about ten o'clock in the morning A. M. on May the 3d, 1863. I am thus particular, Mr. Editor, because it is to be entered on next year's almanac as a remarkable event. The head of the raid did actually arrive at the suburban villa of Mr. Myers, and there it stopped to reconnoitre. There they learned that we had six hundred head of artillery, and six thousand cotton bags, and a permiscuous number of infantry tactics, and we were only waiting to see the whites of their eyes. Also that the history of General Jackson at New Orleans was read in public, and that everybody was inspired to *do something;* whereupon the head of the raid turned pale, and sent forward a picket. At this auspicious moment a foot scout on our side let fly a whistling bullet, which took effect somewhere in those regions. It was reasonably supposed that one Yankee was killed, and perhaps two, for even to this time some thingdead can be smelt in those parts, though the burial squad had not been able to find it up to a late hour yesterday. After right smart skirmishing, the head of the raid fell back down the road to Alabama, and were pursued by our mounted yeomanry at a respectable distance.

Now, Mr. Editor, while all these valiant feats were going on hereabouts, Gen. Forrest had been fighting the body and tail of the raid away down at the Alabama line. Finally he proposed to the raid to stop fighting, and play a game or two of poker, under a cedar tree, which they accepted. But the General was not in luck, and had a poor hand, and staked his last dollar. The Yankees had a *Strait*, which would have taken Forrest and raked down the pile, but he looked 'em right in the eye and said "*he would see 'em and* 4,000 *better.*" The Raid looked at him and he looked at the Raid, and *never blinked.* The Raid trembled all over in his boots, and gave it up. *The General bluffed 'em*, and ever since that game was played the little town close by has been called "*Cedar Bluff.*" It was *flush* times in Alabama, that day, sure.

Well, Mr. Editor, you know the sequel. The General bagged 'em and brought 'em on. The planks were put back on the bridge. The river bank infantry countermarched and fired a promiscuous volley in token of jubilee. One of the side wiping cannon went off on its own hook, and the ball went dead through a house and tore a bureau all to flinders. Some said it was a *Nitre Bureau*, but a potash man who examined said he reckoned not, for there was no ashes in the drawers, nor nary ash hopper on the premises.

By and by, the Camancha scouts and pickets all came in, and shook their ambrosial locks and received the congratulations of their friends. Then begun the ovation of fair women and brave men to Gen. Forrest and his gallant boys. Bouquets and tears were mixed up promiscuous. Big hunks of cake and gratitude were distributed generally and frequent. Strawberries and cream, eggs and onions, pies and pancakes, all flew round amazingly, for everybody was determined to *do something.* Gen. Forrest subsided, and Gen. Jubilee took command, and Rome was herself again. The 4 pronged forks and silver spoons arose from the dead, and even the old hen that one of our city aldermen had buried with her *head out,* was disinterred and sacrificed immediately for the good of the country.

Thus has ended the raid, and no loss on our side. Howsoever, I suppose that Mr. Lincoln will keep "pegging away."

Yours, truly and immensely,

BILL ARP,

Adjective General of Yeomanry.

GEN. FORREST. p. 40.

THE MILITIA OFFICERS REDUCED TO RANKS, AND ORDERED TO SAVANNAH.

The following is the substance of an interview between a "Reduced" and a potash man. It's hard to tell who is ahead.

Potash.—What's the matter, Big John?

Reduced Aid.—Why, nothing particular, only it's darned curious. How in the dickens can Joe Brown reduce a Major to a private, when he hasn't done any thing? What sort of an army regulation do you call that? Joe Brown's new tactics, I reckon. Double barrel shot gun, blanket, haversack, Beauregard, and all that sort of nonsense. Somebody's a fool—a h—l of a fool—and I reckon it's me. I wasn't subject nohow. It's now the rise of 42 years since I come into this cursed old world, but I thought the Confederacy would be calling 'em up to 45 before long, so I took roundence and fudged on 'em and managed to get on one of their ding'd old staffs. Fat and slick; I reckon I was about the last one to get on—no chance to holler "fat and go last."

Durn the staff and Joe Brown too. He played smash amazingly, writing pages against conscription. I thought from the way he pitched into Jeff Davis about trying to enroll his militia officers, that we wouldn't have to fight nothing for the next twenty-five years. Now, you see, he's conscripted the whole concern himself, all at once, in a pile, and reduced 'em all to the ranks. He's a devil of a Governor—Commander-in-Chief. Blame his old hide of him; I'll bet he don't appear at Savannah, not him. Durned if I don't go anywhere he'll risk *his* carcass. Not him.

He turns us all over to old Bory, and old Bory will fight, dog'd if he don't. He'll put just such fellows as me in the front ranks, where David put Goliah, and some of them whistling bullets or singing bombs will take my old gizzard, kerchunk.

Potash.—Well, but John, he ain't going to keep you but a little while.

Reduced.—"Little while! Little while!" you say. Bet my ears if old Bory once gets his French paws on a militia officer, he'll hold him during the war, and fight him some afterwards just for the fun of it. When this fuss is over he will take 'em to Arkansas to fight the Indians. Better believe he hasn't any love for Joe Brown's pets. No, sir; he'll fight 'em hard enough to make up for lost time. Farewell, vain world—when they ain't fighting they'll be digging, and when they ain't digging they'll be fighting. *Little while!* *One day* might be while enough for *my* daylights to be shelled out. I tell you what, when the Yanks get to throwing their blasted hot shot at Savannah, they'll throw 'em thicker and faster than hail ever fell in a cotton patch. Somebody's going to get hurt, sure. Durn old Brown. He is as big a fool on a proclamation as old Abe Lincoln.

Why I thought at first it was a joke, and I looked at the date of the paper, to see if it wasn't the first day of April; then I thought there was some way or other to get out of this business, but blame my old shoes if I see any. I went to see the General, thought maybe he would resist it, or something, but ding it all, I found him in a store buying a haversack, fixing to go. Well, I tried to laugh it off, but it wouldn't laugh. Blamed if every giggle I tried to make didn't fizzle out into a regular whine. Blast Joe Brown, I could enjoy the thing splendidly if I wasn't one of 'em. It's good enough for fellows who were under forty, and who instead of going to fight, slipped under Brown's wagon sheet. Served 'em right. But you see, my time hadn't come—I got skeered too soon—thought once I would put in a substitute, but durn the luck, I don't see any thing about substitutes in this two hundred and forty order. It don't give a man time to know what to do. It just says come along—come quick—be in a hurry—right away—immediately—cars waiting on you—last whistle blow'd—bring shot-gun and blanket—don't look back

—old Beauregard's calling you—enrolling officer after you—court-martial get you—run, run, run like the devil to Savannah. Who ever heard the like of that? It's a snap judgment—blamed if it ain't.

Potash.—Well, John, we must all do our share. You know I've been working for six months as hard as I could, making potash for the Confederacy, and that's to make powder for you boys to fight with.

Reduced.—Potash! yes, potash! Nitre bureau! I'm told that there is about twelve hundred of you fellows skulkin' behind a parcel of ash hoppers, pretending you are stewing down patriotism into powder. Blamed if I can't smell the *lie* on you. You get a government contract for a few thousand pounds, and you fool along with it, selling what you do make to these drug men at a bigger price, and you have twenty-five or thirty on your *personal* staff as partners or workers, and you all go when you please, and come when you please, and stay as long as you please, and you carry your papers wherever you go, just like one of the shipwrecked foreigners that used to travel over the country with a certificate that a volcano had busted and run all over him, and his family was shipwrecked on the Island of Madagasker. Don't you throw your potash in my face; blamed if I am in a humor to put myself on a level with that everlasting nitre bureau. If the men engaged in that business worked half their time, they would make nitre enough in six months to keep forty volcanoes burning two thousand years. "*Everybody do their share*," you say. Blamed if I can't do your share, and nobody ever miss me from this town. I can find all such as you any day, without having to travel a hundred yards. Confound your nitre bureau and your potash; confound old Joe Brown and his durned old staff—blanket, shot gun, Savannah, Beauregard, the devil, * * * Well, I'll be hanged if I don't go. Fact is, I've felt like sucking eggs ever since I got on the durned staff, and may be a little more fighting will make me feel better. (Exit.)

THE MILITIA MAN RETURNED.

DIALOGUE NUMBER TWO.

Potash.—Why, halloa, John, have you got back from Savannah already?

Reduced.—Of course I have—don't you see me—what do you ask such a fool question for? [Puts on martial airs.]

Potash.—I didn't mean no insult, John; I just thought you got back very quick.

Reduced.—Did you suppose it was going to take a year to whip a parcel of blue-bellied Yankees? They knew who was coming after their codfish, and they retired—yes, sir, they evacuated. We have now fallen back to recruit. You see, Jim, we are the reserve. We occupy the post of honor, which you know is the post of danger. We are the "reliable gentlemen," as the editors say. The militia of Georgia now stand conspicuous as the Old Guard of Napoleon Bonaparte, and Joe Brown is old Bony himself come to light—regenerated, resurrected, reconstructed—and I am one of the militia myself, I am. I've been to Savannah, and stood on the ramparts. Talk about your *forty*fications, why there's *a hundred* and forty at Savannah, and more cannon, and bigger ones, than ever was blasted. Blame my eyes, if some of 'em ain't big enough to drive a team in and not tech a hub. I didn't see it tried, Jim, but I'll be dad-swamp'd if the commissary didn't keep his flour in 'em—nine barrels to the gun; that's so, certain and sure. Potash ain't nowhere now, nor overseers, nor shoe-shops, nor travelling preachers, nor details, nor all such. The fact is, we have fought enough to balance off nine square miles of your potash woods. Jim, you ought to join the militia.

Potash.—Look here, John, your talk don't suit me. I ain't no fool if I am making *potash.* I've done as much fighting as you, and I haven't done *any.* "*Fought enough,*" you say! Well, John, you ain't the first *staff* officer that bragged about his fighting. I once heard a big fat fellow in a theatre, by the name of Fal-*staff*, do the same thing, and he got caught at it. Now let me advise you to sing low about this fighting business. Me and you are about even on the goose question. I don't consider you ahead by no means, for old Brown will get you in a close place yet.

Reduced.—Look here, Jim, hush; I know I can't fool you; blame my skin if I wasn't joking. The boys all talked that way, and I followed suit. Durn that luck, I ain't no fool myself, and I know we ain't out of the woods. Joe Brown just called us to Savannah to see how docile we were. Well, we got to Atlanta, and he said "*halt*," and we halted. Then he said "counter-march—go home," and we got ready for the cars in double-quick. Then he cried out, "*counter-march to Savannah*," and to Savannah we went *straight forthwith*. Now here we are again, but where we will be day after to-morrow, no mortal fool knows except Joe Brown. Blame the militia. Dad burn old Brown. What security has a man got for his liberty? What satisfaction is there in living between hawk and buzzard? Who cares about travelling on the railroad when every impertinent dog on the way can stand off and point and say, "Thar go the Melish; yonder come the Melish; do you see that Melish?" when I knew the contemptible curse had a substitute in the army himself, or was overseeing twenty negroes, or carrying on a little shoe shop, or stewing down potash, or—

Potash.—Look here, John, you've said enough about potash, just dry that up!

Reduced.—Jim, I will curse the potash, blamed if I ain't got a right to curse everybody and every thing that ain't fighting. I get off in Billy Smith's woods and curse myself regular. I can whip any thing that stays at home. We will have a race of people after a while that ain't worth

BIG JOHN ORDERED TO SAVANNAH. p. 43.

a curse. The good ones are getting killed up, but these *skulkers* and *shirkers* and *dodgers* don't die. There ain't one died since the war broke out. Confound 'em, dod rot 'em; I begin to believe our old devil is dead; if he ain't, he's no account or he'd have had some of these fellows before now. Wonder if Brown would let me go and fight awhile under the Confederacy? But then I would be in for the war, and I don't like that. Durned if I know what to do—I'm still on the durned staff. Hanged if I know whether I've got my commission or my commission has me. Jim, I'm just in old Scoggins' fix.

Potash.—How's that, John?

Reduced.—Well, you see old Scoggins got so drunk in town he couldn't navigate his steers; so he drove out in the edge of the woods and got out of the wagon and laid down by a tree to sleep the drunk off. He woke up about midnight, and his steers were gone, but the wagon was there. His brain was still so fuddled that he didn't know who he was, nor how he come there; so he thought over as well as he could, and finally extemporized, "Am I John Scoggins, or am I not John Scoggins? If I am John Scoggins, I've lost a yoke of steers; but if I ain't John Scoggins, I'll be d—d if I haven't found a wagon." Now, Jim, that's my fix. I don't know my *situation*, as the editors head their war talk. Sometimes I think I have lost a yoke of steers, and then again I conclude that I have found a wagon.

Potash.—Well, John, let me ask you how long does a commission run before it runs out?

Reduced.—Why it runs forever and ever, and a few days over, unless you run yourself, and that's the only way you can run out of your commission; and you can get court-martialed for that and shot. This here court-martial business is a powerful strain on a man. It is like *tare* and *tret* in the old Federal Calculator. I tried to look as big as Gen. Jackson, and went up to a lawyer, and says I, "I'll be hanged if I'm going to Savannah. What can Joe Brown do with me? what's the law?" Says he, "Gov. Brown will court-martial you, and may be will condemn you to be shot." "Well," said I, "but I will appeal, and then I'll get you to carry the case to the Supreme Court, and keep it in law till the fuss is over." Said he, "We can't carry it there; lawyers are not allowed to practise in Military Courts. Gov. Brown is the head of the court. He is the Supreme Court himself." So you see, Jim, I collapsed. Blame such a court. Joe Brown orders me to jail; I appeal to a special jury, and Joe Brown is the jury. I carry it to the Supreme Court, and Joe Brown is the court. Blame my neck if a man didn't get hung *twice* going through that programme. Hang the thing. It's all on one side, just like an Atlanta Hotel. Brown's got us, and I reckon it's the best plan to humor the joke. "*Hurrah for the Militia,*" that's the way to talk it. "*Three cheers for Joe Brown,*" that's the way to say it. Pat him on the back, and tell him the militia are for him! that's the way to do it. Blamed if I don't write him a love letter to-night on the success of the militia at Savannah.

Jim, give me a chew of tobacco.

A MESSAGE TO ALL FOLKS.

Standing on the seat of a split-bottom chair, I exclaim, in the language of Dan Rice, Esq., "F-e-l-l-e-r-sitizens!"

Being much gratified for your distinguished consideration which has been showered down upon me like an avalanche in times past, and heretofore, and before now, and previous, I desire to attract your attention on this posthumous occasion.

In the first place and firstly, I deem it my duty to inform you that the Devil is to pay, and he won't rcceive Confederate money. It is therefore highly necessary for the people to get together and take some action on the

CURRENCY BILL.

My opinion having been solicited by all mankind and some few others, and asked for with tremendous anxiety by everybody else, I have made it up with great care, and done it up in a Georgia rag. Out of curiosity I have weighed it, and find it is heavy—very heavy—weighing some thirteen pounds, more or less, and being an opinion as is an opinion.

To relieve the public distress, I therefore proceed to state, that the late Currency Bill is believed to be that great and most monstrous maelstrom which the geographers describe as abounding on the coast of Norway, but which by some jugglery or hocus pocus or secret session has recently been bought and moved into the Confederacy, to swallow up all the money in circulation. With a kind of whirligig locomotion, it is drawing the currency into its awful and greedy vortex, leaving a man nothing to remind him of it but sickly scrap of yellow paper, which has been daguerretóyped from a hospital flag. This Bill is the kill-devil of all trade, and ought to exasperate all those patriotic citizens who hold their truck for higher prices, as they will lose by it perhaps.

My opinion is, that some other Bill might have been found that would have done better or worse. One might have been discovered on the coast of Africa, or in the Lake of Good Hope, or somewhere in the Mediterranean Mountains, but Congress was, I suppose, afraid to run the blockade after it. If they had applied to your distinguished and humble fellow-citizen, I would have undertaken the job. But, alas! they didn't. On the contrary, they barred the doors, and shut the window blinds, and let down the curtains, and stopped up the keyholes, and went into a place called

SECRET SESSION,

which is perhaps a little the closest communion ever established in a well-watered country. A grand jury or a Masonic Lodge, or a Know-Nothing convention, isn't a circumstance to it. It is a thing that plots, and plans, and schemes for a few weeks, and then suddenly pokes its head out like a catawampus and says, *Booh!* Then all the pop-eyed folks run about and say, *Booh! Booh!!* And the peaceable, *anti-bullet* citizens begin to tremble in the knees, and say, *Booh! Booh!! Booh!!!* And it keeps travelling faster and faster, and growing bigger and bigger, until it reaches the Governor, and he is constrained to get on a fodder-stack pole and say in a loud voice, *Booh! Booh!! Booh!!! Booh!!!! B-o-o-o-o-o-o-h!!!!!*

It was in this dark and benighted hole that a plan was set on foot to procure a fierce and rambunkshus animal from the mountains of Hepsidam, and having starved him for several days, they suspended him to a swinging limb in the President's yard, and locked his chain with Mr. Hobbs's lock, and gave Mr. Davis the key. Some ten thousand years ago, more or less, this animal was discovered by King Charles the Second, and named with the name of

HABEAS CORPUS.

It is, perhaps, *when suspended*, the most savagerous beast that ever got after tories and traitors. To all honest and patriotic folks it is said to be perfectly harmless, but still, nevertheless, notwithstanding, howsomever, *it might get loose*, and waylay our liberties, and tear the hind sights off a man, before he could bellow for help. Its nose is said to be a perfect olfactory, and for miles and miles, across rivers, and swamps, and prairies, and piney woods, it smells out all such as would ferment discord, and spread disaffection among the people. When a man or set of men do make themselves into a gridiron, and begin to broil the peace and harmony of the country, this animal does snuff the tainted atmosphere, and try to break his chain.

F-E-L-L-E-R-CITIZENS: The war, and the Yankees, and old Lincoln and his threats of subjugation, extermination, amalgamation, desolation, and Mr. Toombs' foul domination, is a big thing, terrible and horrible. But old Habeas *hung up*, and secret sessions, and the currency bill, and conscription, are far bigger, and awful in the extreme. Our soldiers ought to let the Yankees alone, and come home and fight these savage beasts, and you, my fellow-citizens, ought to arm yourselves with sticks, and rocks, and thrashpoles, and hot water, and pikes, and make a violent assault upon these "most monstrous paradoxes."

I must express my astonishment that you are all so quiet and unconscious—that you are so blind as not to see the danger that hangs like a Boa constrictor over you.

I feel like you will always, and evermore, and a good while afterwards, be under everlasting obligations to me for standing guard over your sleeping liberties, like a crane upon a sand-hill, or a sentinel upon the Lamp post of Freedom. Overcome by my emotions on this august occasion, allow me to intersperse before you a paragraph of

POETRY.

"I wish I was the President of these Confederate States,
I'd eat sugar and candy and swing upon the gates."

And this brings me to consider for your edification the

CONSCRIPTION BILL,

which has so long deprived you of the right to volunteer, and like a vampire gnawed away at your burning and glowing patriotism.

Looking through the horn of my imagination, methinks I see this Bill repealed, and all the people of Georgia (that are not in the war), both old and young, and big and little, rushing to the front in one glorious phalanx, to offer up their lives on the altar of liberty.

Methinks I see them, as in a horn, crowding the road, and swimming the rivers, and climbing the mountains, exclaiming with majestic fury—

"We come, we come—ye have called us long—
We come o'er the mountings—in a horn."

But I forbear, fellow-citizens, to rankle your feelings by recounting all the outrages which the grand Catawampus at Richmond has perpetrated upon you.

Awaiting your thanks and adulations, I would now subside into my seat, if I was through my message. But I must expatiate somewhat on the

CAUSE OF THE WAR.

Some folks say it was the Abolishonists who got up this fuss. *Some say they didn't.* Some say it was politicians, and some it was a supernatural thing called *Manifest Destiny.* Some are of the opinion that the *nigger* was at the bottom of it, and that ever since the Romans carried the war into Africa, Africa has carried it everywhere else. But, my fellow-citizens, it was caused exclusively by Gen. States Rights going to sleep one day, and old Colonel Federalist come along, and tried to cut his ham-string. I am for the General as long as I am on his staff, and I am going to pitch into the Colonel on every possible occasion. So now you understand what brought about the war.

Fellow-citizens, do you want peace? Are you tired of this struggle? Then let me tell you my plan of making

PROPOSITIONS FOR PEACE.

After every victory over our enemies, let us holler at the top of our voices peace! peace!! peace!!! In the language of Patrick Henry, let us cry "Peace when there is no peace." What we shall holler after every *defeat* this deponent sayeth not, and would like for you to say yourself if you know.

I am aware that Mr. Davis in his message, and Congress in their addresses, and our generals in their official communications, have all the time entreated our enemies to let us alone, to let us have peace; and I am also aware that the Constitution says that Congress *alone* should have the right to declare war and make peace, but *nevertheless notwithstanding*, I have got a right to holler *enough!* or *peace! peace!* if I want to, and I am going to do it!

I am now about to bring this important message to a close. My ostensible object in addressing you was the "Currency Bill," which only gives the great State of Georgia until Christmas to fund her money in six per cent. bonds.

Fearing that the Legislature might get all killed up before their regular sessions, I have thought proper to agitate the subject *now*, and bring before you all the other "Monstrous Paradoxes," as side shows to the circus.

Calling your attention to the appendix which follows, I now descend from my chair, and having taken a chaw of tobacco, subscribe myself your fellow-citizen,

BILL ARP.

APPENDIX TO HABEAS CORPUS.

Since the discovery of America by Pocahontas, the *habeas corpus* has never been suspended over anybody, except about three hundred thousand soldiers in the Confederate army. For nearly three years, General Lee and Johnston have had it suspended over all the fighting boys in their commands. With most astonishing patience they bear up under this oppression, and continue to live on half rations and fight, and march, and toil, and struggle, and *never complain about nothing.* I asked some of them how they got along with the *habeas corpus* hanging over them, and they said "I was a fool," and called me a "*damn'd old Gogge*,"* or some such name. If I was governor I would send missionaries among them immediately.

BILL ARP.

* Bill must have misunderstood the soldiers. They probably said "*Demagogue.*"—ED.

BILL ARP'S LETTER TO HIS OLD FRIEND JOE.

MY DEAR OLD JOE: You know I call you *old*, because you have got along so fast since I first knew you. You have played your cards (I don't mean your cotton cards) mighty well heretofore, but somehow you seem to have lost ground lately. May be you are trying to get ahead of the wagon. I'm mighty sorry I couldn't be at your big convention and advise with you a little. I might possibly have pulled you back *some* and hurt your feelings, but it would have been the best in the long run, and saved you a power of mortification.

You used to write to me for advice, Joe, and you always succeeded when you followed it, but this time you didn't even ask me for my opinion, but just wrote me to go and see the members in the adjoining counties—let 'em know what was on hand, and get 'em properly roused up for the great occasion that was to come off. Well, Joe, I was afraid the plan wouldn't work; I was dubious of it certain, but I done what you said, and talked to 'em about that "*habeas corpus*" until some of 'em were excited amazingly. It was late one evening when I got to Dick's house. I found Dick ploughing away down in a field close by a sweet-gum swamp, and when I got through talking to him, he would not have stayed in that field till dark for a thousand dollars. So thinks I, says I, if *I* can scare Dick that bad, what might I not expect of you, Joe?

I was then satisfied you had the Legislature dead.

Well, Joe, I don't know all that was done at your convention, for I was not there, but I'll tell you what, old feller, Linton played his part of the programme *jam up*. I heard one of the members say that after Linton got through his big speech that night, some of 'em was so scared of the old *habeas corpus*, they kept looking around behind 'em, like we boys used to do, when the negroes were telling us ghost stories. Some of 'em boarded at private houses, and they didn't go home *that night*, but slept about at the hotels with the other members. You see, Joe, when Linton said, "Who knows but what the President has already got his secret police around this capitol? Who knows but what he may *this night* be grappled forth from his peaceful repose, and in a moment, in the tinkling of an eye, be hurried off to 'that barn from whence no traveller returns'?" That got 'em; Dick says when Linton said that, the silence was so immense, you could have heard a flea jump in the saw-dust on the floor, if there had been one in the house. Lint played his cards well—(I do not allude to your cotton cards, Joe).

Well, Joe, you must have had a heap of trouble. There was some powerful difficulties in your way, certain. In the first place, the *time* was of very doubtful propriety. If you had only waited until the President *had took up somebody* with the "*habeas corpus*," and collapsed him in the caverns of a secret dungeon, you would have had more capital to work on. You know, Joe, you had until Christmas anyhow, to fund the State's money, so I can't see what put you in such an everlasting hurry.

Sometimes I think you are trying to climb too fast, Joe. You see your ideas get so much elevation that your head gets dizzy and your brain begins to swim, and you naturally overlook some things and commit indiscretions which are distressing. Now there is your old neighbor who thinks mighty well of you, and always votes right; but when I told him your programme about calling the convention, he appeared astonished most powerful—said it was all a humbug and wouldn't pay, and he was afraid you would break your neck a-paving your way to the Presidency. He didn't approve your resolutions which you wanted the convention to pass, but said if you succeeded in having them put through, especially that one censuring Mr. Davis, he would furnish you with another set to have passed immediately afterwards. He requested me enclose them to you, which I will do. They are as follows, to wit:

Resolutions to be passed, peaceably if I can, forcibly if I must, bolus noxshus, anyhow.

First. *Be it enacted*, That I am a whale, and if there is any bigger fish a-swimming in the nasty deep, then I am *that.*

Secondly. *Resolved*, That Richmond is Jonah, and will be swallowed up in a few days—in a few days—Shanghai chickens they grow tall in a few days. (Joe is to stand on a box and sing this song immediately after this resolution is passed.)

Thirdly. *Resolved*, That whereas some ignorant poet has asked, What constitutes a State? he is informed that *it's me;* I am the State myself.

Fourthly. *Resolved*, That I am the centre of space—the Southern Confederacy—the solar system—the mariner's compass—the card factory—equinoctial gale—the almanac, with all its eclipses—the undiscovered perpetual motion—the State Road—the locomotive engine, with the steam up—in fact, if there is any other big thing, then I am that.

I asked him if he was not a-joking—a-playing off a little burlesque—and he said, No; that you could pass 'em if you could pass yours, and he didn't know but what you would try it anyhow. He told me to tell you to mind how you played your cards. (He didn't mean the cotton-cards.)

And there, Joe—right there—oh, my dear old Joe,

them cards—them *cotton*-cards—there's where you missed it. Dick told me all about that, and though he voted for you, he said he didn't like the looks of it—you ought to have sent them cards off about a month before to the members, to distribute to the soldiers' families. They need 'em mighty bad, and you know it. But you sold 'em to the members at ten dollars a pair, *just on the heel of voting time.* It may have been all right, Joe, but somehow the two things come off in very dangerous proximity. I hardly think it got you any votes, for the members didn't feel like it was any favor from you, for the cards (I mean the cotton-cards, Joe) was as much theirs as yours; that is to say, they didn't belong to any of you, unless, as your neighbor says in the resolution, "You are the State!" Joe, I have frequently thought how much good them cards would have done the poor soldiers' families in this country. But this is not the worst of it. Dick says you allowed the members to exchange two hundred dollars of Confederate money for two hundred dollars of State money, "even steven," and also to change the same amount for Georgia change bills, and they were paid off their salaries besides in State money (which last was all right, of course). Why, Joe—my old Joe—my foolish Joe—my inconsiderate fellow, What was you thinking about? Have you just turned out to regular bribing, and that with other people's money? It's bad enough to do it with one's own money; but, my aspiring friend, what will the people say about it?

Joe, my dear Joe, you must surely have misconstructed the "Funding Act." It didn't provide for no such funding as that. Do come up and see me. I want to talk to you—I am afraid you have forgotten your first lesson of propriety. Surely, surely, there is some mistake about this, but Dick says not, and he showed me his money and cards (I mean cotton-cards). He says he wouldn't have took his, but he heard a member say that if the Governor was that loose with the State property, the more they took from him the better.

I am afraid you are losing ground, Joe, and I don't blame you for circulating your message in handbills, but there are some things you must keep as dark as possible. Don't mention the *cotton-cards* in your appendix—keep your newspapers straight. I noticed that your Augusta organ replied to the "Savannah Republican" about the card business. This was very indiscreet—you must write to him and learn him better—smother it—squash it—drown it—*nol pros.* it, *if possible.*

In conclusion, Joe, I hope you won't let them resolutions complimenting Jeff. Davis affect you too much. You say in your letter that "it shocked you." Never mind that—let 'em shock on. If they will shock some of your foolishness out of you, it will do you good. Quit writing so much—your messages are too long—especially for a call-session. There is no use in it, and besides paper is high and ink scarce. Haul in a little—bide your time. It's not everybody that can get to be President. My candid opinion is, that you will make a mighty good Governor if you will stick to it a few more terms. Solomon says "there is a place for every thing, and a thing for every place," and Don Quixote says "that every dog has his day." Write to me, Joe, and do tell me all that you *did* do in trying to pass them resolutions. I am afraid I have not heard the half of it.

Your old friend,

BILL ARP.

P. S.—About that money business, let me ask you, "Will you be able to balance up your books to a quarter of a cent, and show *no loss on our side?*" B. A.

THE QUARTERMASTER'S LAMENT.

Horses and wagons and mules, barracks and quarters and tents,
Axes and shovels and tools, hire and niggers and rents;
Coats and breeches and shoes, haversacks, blankets and hats,
Nails and iron and screws, pontoons and bridges and flats;
Fuel and kettles and plank, envelopes, paper and ink,
Till the abstract I'm filling looks blank, and my brain is too dizzy to
think,
Will there never be an end to this everlasting issue?
Will the time never come when the Gen'l wouldn't miss you,
If some day you steal away, in a solitude to stay,
Where the horses draw no forage and the officers no pay?

HILTON—Hilton, M. C. Is he a bird or a buzzard? I'm a poor carcass of a quartermaster, lean and lantern-jawed, pretty nigh dead with service, weary and worn; and Hilton has come to torment me before my time. Would he pick my bones before I am cold? Does he want me branded, like a worn-out army horse, with the letter "C?" Where did Mr. Hilton fly from when he lit upon that light-house at Richmond? I never heard of him until I read his wholesale bill of indictment against Quartermasters and Commissaries. He must be from Arkansaw, I reckon, or some other part unknown. My daddy sold goods on credit about forty years ago, and when a customer run away, he used to codicil his name with "G. T. A.," *gone to Arkansaw.* What a power of dead heads must have roosted in them woods on the other side of Jordan! If Hilton, M. C., did fly from those parts, I'll wager a dead horse that he got a powerful vote from that class who figured on my old daddy's books. It is a bad sign for a man to be pitchin' into a class of people, and calling the whole of 'em thieves and swindlers, just because he's heard of a rascal or two among 'em; might just as well call the whole Congress a fool because they've got a fool among 'em. Monsieur Hilton, M. C., wants all us removed from office, and put in the ranks, and our places supplied by civilians who are over age and under size, and physically unable to do field service; wants a lot of sickly, tallow-faced gentlemen, who've got the gout, or the blind-piles, or the sore back, or the belchin' dispepsy, or the grubbs, or the Chinese diarrhœa, or the big shoulder, or the painter's colic, or the botts, or the string-halt, or the sway back, and all that sort of thing.

Here we've worked day and night, in the mud and in the rain, loading and unloading, pressing and being pressed, scolding and being scolded, paying out and paying in, hunting horses, hunting niggers, hunting forage, and wagons, and harness, and beef, and bacon, and flour, and supplies; run almost to death under the responsibility of keeping our corner up, feeling all the time like a poor galley slave, and yet no word of approval; no look of reward; no vote of thanks; no brief editorial from the press; no small scrap of praise from "P. W. A." or "N'Importe," or "Personne" or any army corrrespondent!

The fact is, Mr. Hilton, M. C. & Company have set the dogs on us. It's good Buncombe to have a scape-goat! Mr. Buncombe can go home and say, "Didn't I give them Quartermasters and Commissaries fits? I saved the Government several millions of dollars." Well, it's very strange that all the rascals managed to get into these departments. Heap of them I knew before the war who were considered gentlemen and honest, have somehow or other been sworn, chosen, and selected by somebody as fit and proper persons for disbursing officers. But Hilton & Co. are after 'em, and Congress have sorter compromised the fuss by our increasing bonds to fifty thousand dollars! What a humbug! What a "*brutem fulmen*," as the feller said, which in dog Latin they say signifies a *foolish brute!* Don't they know that a quarter of a million passes through my hands in a year? What's the bond worth, if I am going into a regular stealin' business? It would be a plagued sight more sensible if they had abolished all the bonds, and put a man fairly and squarely upon his honor; and if he violated his honor, or stole a dollar directly or indirectly, why, let his General hang him up at the cross roads where the army could see him, and let him hang there high and dry in the cold and the wet, in the wind and the rain, until his flesh dried up, and his shirt-tail wore out a-flappin' in the pitiless storm.

That's the way old Bonaparte done 'em, and it's the only way; don't you know it is? Why, in a regular war like this, there ain't no system of checks or counter-checks, or balances, or safeguards, that will insure honesty in these departments. Suppose my blacksmiths work up two thousand pounds of iron a week into horse-shoes, crow-bars, and fifth-chains, and I have 'em made *light*, and issue them out by number, and give myself credit for three thousand pounds; who's to know any better when the shoes are worn out, and the chains are broke and thrown away? Suppose a battle is *imminent*, as they say, and I send forward wagons and ambulances, and axes and shovels, and after the battle is over, I enter up twice the amount as *lost in battle*, and my General thinks I'm honest, and signs the certificate? Talk about your bonds! Why, those three letters L. I. B. will hide a multitude of sins, and cover up three months of fraud and rascality. Then there's the goods taken from the enemy—leather and shoes, horses and blankets, and jeans, that comes into my possession without any invoice or descriptive list—I pick out and box up and ship off to sell "*on account of whom it may concern.*"

Alas, Mr. Hilton, M. C., I fear you can't fix it up. If you have got your heart set on it, you are in my old lawyer friend Hardin's fix who got his heart set on the *bench*, but poor fellow, he was never able to set any thing else on the bench. You had just as well git sick and quit. We don't feel like payin' our taxes to pay you for your wastin' our time. Try your hand on something you know more about, and when you've succeeded and give us evidence of your usefulness, just git on a stump if you please, and holler out as loud as you can bawl, "*Here's the place to git your money back!*" Make a big thing of it, Mr. Hilton, when you holler, so that we can all hear you and rejoice.

But then, after all, we've got some comfort. Our Generals appreciate us; the army officers with whom we transact our business, stand by us, and look down with curly-nosed contempt on all such jackassism. How comforting it was to hear General Polk remark the other day, "My corps is ready for action; every thing is complete; my quartermasters and commissaries and surgeons have been most diligent and energetic; in fact, I have ceased to feel any apprehension about their departments." And how consoling to hear that other eloquent remark from a trafficking Shylock of a French-German-Jew, "I tot I could make some of de monish here 'mong dese officere, but by tam, dese quartermasters too tam hones; I do nothin' wid dem."

Mr. Buncombe, if you'll move to our district, we'll run that Shylock against you for Congress the next term.

BILL ARP.

DODGING AROUND—MELANCHOLY REFLECTIONS.

Farmer with a dog-skin.—"Just look at that, will you, and price it?—fattest dog-skin you ever saw—what'll you give for it?"

Tanner.—"Don't want it—don't buy fat dog-skins, they are always rotten."

Farmer.—"Well, now—come to think of it, I was joking—the dog wasn't so blame fat as you might suppose. I'll be darn'd if he didn't starve to death."

And that's nature—human nature. It ain't dog nature, nor cow nature, nor horse nature: but it's human nature just dodging around. I am a poor judge of Scripture. I don't know how good our forefathers were when old Uncle Adam was gardening on the Eufrates river, but my opinion is that man has fallen. If he ain't, then animals have risen—brutes have got better or people worse, and no mistake. In fact, I'd rather risk animals. My horse don't fool me, nor my cow, nor my sheep; and if my coon dog does sometimes bark up the wrong tree, he don't mean any harm by it, and there is nothing that wears breeches that's half so honest as the wag of my dog's tail.

Folks are not reliable. If one is so occasionally, it is an exception. He is looked upon as a curiosity, and his remarkable conduct gets in the papers, and is narrated and narrated about as an extraordinary circumstance. If he pays up his old debts that are gone out of date, it is considered a sort of a miracle, and goes dodging around for a heap more than it's worth—more than likely he broke at first and got rich at last by tricking and trapping and dodging around. If I could see him give in his taxes, and didn't smell perjury, he could stand fire and smoke. Old Diogenes might blow out his candle, and hunt no more for an honest man. There's the time and the place, and the circumstance that tries a man's soul. Just watch him and study him as he gives in his taxes—see the flinching and squirming and dodging around, for this here anno domini 1863 is powerful hard on the root of all evil. There's the city tax, and the county tax, and State tax, and Confederate tax, and general tax, and special tax, and church tax, and charity tax, and tax in kind, and tax unkind, and shoe tax, and salt tax, and speculator's tax in general; and they scourge a man hard, and they scourge him frequent, and poor human nature caves in. The day a man gives in his taxes he is poorer than any day in the year, and it would not be wrong to assert that a country is richer by fifty per cent. than its taxes foot up. This deficit ought to be a column by itself, and charged up to perjury or dodging around.

There's Snooks, who didn't give in his young niggers, because he said they were no profit to him. Old Shirk wouldn't give in his notes because the stay law wouldn't let him collect 'em, and they might prove insolvent before they were paid. Old Dodge gave his money to his wife a few days before the first day of April. Old Grab has been sued for his niggers, and now won't give 'em in because the case ain't determined. Old Gitall bought his salt at twenty-five cents, and won't give it in any more because he ain't sold it, and it might go down. Old Crib cuts down his corn about half, for he makes an allowance for rotage, ratage, shrinkage, draggage, lossage, and stealage. Old Hooks's land is worth a cool hundred thousand, but he returns it at thirty, because he says it don't make any more truck than it used to. And there's all mankind in general who are twisting and shirking, and give in their property at a heap too little, for fear of making it a little too much. Gee whilikens, Juba; what a fortune I could make by buying folks' property at their own valuation; what a power of perjury is to be tried or confessed on the other side of Jordan; what a criminal docket; what a power of travelling to those sultry, sulphury regions, where shade-trees don't grow, and there ain't no chance to be dodging around!

But this prolonged war has produced more sublime specimens, more various fashions of dodging around. Of late it has been my high privilege to observe the cavalry—the horse cavalry, which ever and anon migrates and variagates and perambulates through and through a bleeding country. They are perhaps the most majestic sight that belong to the animal kingdom, and such are the profound impression which their august presence do make upon a close observer, that one week's view will satisfy his whole curiosity for the next fifty years to come. Their brilliant appearance is far too powerful for weak eyes to endure more than about seven days in the year. The infantry and artillery is called the two arms of the service, and do very well in their places, but the horse cavalry are the two legs—they are the engine of locomotion, the wheels of progress, and hence can travel better and retire quicker and occupy a heap more ubiquity. If a philosopher wishes to see the perfection and beauty of animal motion, let him get on a mountain and observe the horse cavalry as they wind about the fields, and the farms, and the gardens, the orchards, the corn-patches, and potato-patches, the bee-gums and chicken-coops, and he will be filled with admiration and astonishment at the way they go dodging around. The sleight and rapidity with which they perform their evolutions, are said to be accomplished by their peculiar drill, which is called damning—they dam their eyes, and they dam their ears, and they dam their guns, and their boots, and their mill-saw spurs, and they dam their horses to make 'em go faster, and they dam the fences to make 'em come down, and they dam the poor farmer to make him dry up: hence, I am told that Major Mike Makin always speaks of 'em as the "DAM CAVALRY," which expression might be considered impolite, but the Major has a way of saying it so flat and long that of course he intends it to be eulogistic. What curious ideas of recruiting they have got! Here they were sent to recruit their horses and rest 'em, and strengthen 'em, and you can see 'em at it by day and by night, in an everlasting gallop, going whippity-whoppity, flippity-floppity, just dodging around all over the land. It has been thought that our county court done the biggest road business of any similar road factory in the State; but if a man can travel any big road, or any little road, new road, or old road, public road or private road, any mill path or still-house path, any cow trail, or hog trail, and not meet from two to ten of the d-a-m cavalry, then their camp had been moved some three days before. It takes 'em at least that long to quit a good country after they have left it, for they are at it, and on it, and in it, and around it, and over it, and under it, till it seems like they have to sluff off, like a scab on a sore-back mule. Grand, gloomy, and peculiar, as Bonaparte said, they go dodging around. Gloomy to those who have something they want, and very peculiar as they carry it off. Swapping horses is a weakness to which they are subject, but they give a man very little trouble that way, for they can swap with him when he ain't at home, or when he's asleep, just as well as if he was awake and was there.

But hurrah for the cavalry! When a big battle has been fought, and the enemy got whipped, how majestic they appear as they follow up the skedaddlers, what sublime manœuvres they have on such occasions! It was at such a time I suppose Solomon writ about 'em and said "he snuffeth the battle afar off." When they are pursuing a panic-struck enemy, or laying in wait for a train of cars, or assaulting an ungarded caravan of wagons, the Confederate horse cavalry may be said to be invincible. On such occasions they load themselves down with dry goods, and wet goods, and blankets, and hats, and boots and booty, and ticklers, and canteens with contents noticed. I once heard a poor infantry say as he was hunting over the ground he fought, "Let's go home, Jim, the cavalry have been here and licked up every d-a-m thing—after we whipped the fight here, they come just ripping and snorting, and dodging around."

But taxes and cavalry stand aside, for they can't compete with that numerous class who are dodging conscription. They've kept out so long, and worked so hard to stay out still longer, and sweat so much in dodging around, and they've read so much of big battles, and of so much flesh and blood, and such horrible carnage, that the bare sight of an enrolling officer gives 'em a heart palpitation. They can't sleep for imagining that the screech owl is screaming, and the boomerang howling their funeral dirge; that their bones are to bleach in some gully, or to rot in some thicket, far, far away, where ghosts and boogers go dodging around. How rapidly some folks grow old in these trying times—what a prolific year for boy children it was in the year 1817! Such is the rapid progress of human events in these fighting times, that a man who was only forty last year, can be forty-six this. Even old Father Time has put on his spurs, and now he goes dodging around.

There's the mail must be carried, the telegraph attended to, steamboats and cars must travel, shoes must be made, potash be burnt, and all mechanics must go ahead; and then there's the numerous holes and hiding-places around a depot, or hospital, or the Quartermaster's department, or the passport office, etc., but the bulk of the dodging is done in the chronic line. Before this developing war, it was not thought possible for so much rheumatics and chronics, so many sore legs and weak backs, to exist in a limestone country. Oh! if I was a doctor, how I would dose 'em, and drug 'em, and fill 'em with ipecac! I would quit my general practice, and put out a shingle with "chronics" painted in large letters on it. If I was the Congress, they should be compelled to come to my office at least twice a week, and be blistered, and physicked, and cupped. I would cure 'em or kill 'em, and then our poor, bleeding country would have sound men or none; and that's the way to stop dodging around.

Yours,

B. A.

LETTER FROM BILL ARP.

ROME, GA., *March* 4, 1864.

MR. INTELLIGENCER—

SIR: Being prodigiously bothered about the currency, I presume to ask you for some information. In these regions it appears that all mankind, including free niggers, and niggers expecting to be free, are split up into two classes—those that know something, and those that know nothing—one of whom I am which.

The great question which agitates us now is, "must I fund my money or not," and if not, what shall I do with it? Therefore being in a sort of fog myself, I desire you to answer the following interrogatories consecutively. As follows, namely, viz., to wit—If 8 per cent. bonds and 7.30 notes are taxed 5 per cent. by the new bill, what made 'em jump up instead of jumping down the day the bill was published? Why are they better than 4 per cent. bonds which are not taxed at all? Again—can you fund any sum under a hundred dollars, and if you cannot, what is a fellow to do who has got only ninety dollars? If he cannot *fun* it, will there be any fun in losing thirty of it?

Again—is it possible for the soldiers who are afar off, and their families that don't take the papers, to find out in time how to fund their money, and where to fund it? Won't the five dollar bills that are now hid out come forth like a bear, and lick up the tens and twenties at a heavy discount? Again—suppose I spend four hundred dollars, and get a certificate to that effect, how am I going to buy five bushels of corn with it? Who is to make the change? Again—how long before enough of the new currency can get out to do the business of the country? Can the Government pay out more than a million a day, and will it not be a long period of time before any of it gets to my house? Again—was this bill intended to *raise* the price of trade and trucks, or to *fall* it? If the latter, please inform me what commodity is getting cheaper, and I will buy some of it, and let the funding slide. If you say so, I will send you my pile, with instructions to invest in the first thing that gets down to the price it was the first day the bill was published. It makes no difference whether it is goobers or grindstones, sugar or salt, fine combs or curry-combs, or honeycombs—just pitch in freely and promiscuously—bet it on some bob-tail nag if you want to.

Well, Mr. Editor, as I have remarked, there is an extensive class who does not know any thing about these abstract things, one of whom I am which; but it does seem to be a funny bill. Congress must have had a funny time over it in secret session. No wonder it is to take effect on the funniest day in the year, and by the time we all get through funding our funds, there will be more April fools than my rooster can crow at.

It is whispered around in select circles (and that is how I came to hear it), that this bill would not have passed, but Mr. Memminger lost his account-book when they had the last big scare in Richmond, and he informed Congress that there was no way to tell how much money was out, without calling it all in again. He was asked to say about how much he thought was in circulation; and he said he hadn't charged his memory particularly, but according to his recollection there was *six hundred millions* or *six thousand millions*—he was not certain which.

Mr. Editor, will you write to me and give me your peculiar views on the currency, and advise me what to do with my money? If you was me, and didn't have but four hundred dollars, and could buy eggs that was laid after the 13th day of February, wouldn't you buy them? Methinks I hear you answer in the language of Othello—"*Eggsactly.*"

Yours,

BILL ARP.

P. S.—Tip is my peculiar institution, and he says he

feels a peculiar interest in the currency, and would like to know as how, supposing a gentleman desire him to illuminate his boots, or amputate his wood-pile, will the gentleman fork over a bond, or just say "thankee," or how? He talks about selling his axe.

B. A.

BILL ARP, THE ROMAN RUNAGEE.

ATLANTA, GA., MAY 22, 1864.

MR. EDITOR: "Remote, unfriended, melancholy, slow," as somebody said, I am seeking a log in some vast wilderness, a lonely roost in some Okeefenokee swamp, where the foul invaders cannot travel nor their pontoon bridges float. If Mr. Shakspeare were correct when he wrote that "sweet are the juices of adversity," then it is reasonable to suppose that me and my folks, and many others, must have some sweetening to spare. When a man is aroused in the dead of night, and smells the approach of the foul invader; when he feels constrained to change his base and become a runagee from his home, leaving behind him all those ususary things which hold body and soul together; when he looks, perhaps the last time, upon his lovely home where he has been for many delightful years raising children and chickens, strawberries and peas, lye soap and onions, and all such luxuries of this sublunary life; when he imagines every unusual sound to be the crack of his earthly doom; when from such influences he begins a dignified retreat, but soon is constrained to leave the dignity behind, and get away without regard to the order of his going—if there is any sweet juice in the like of that, I haven't been able to see it. No, Mr. Editor, such scenes never happened in Bill Shakspeare's day, or he wouldn't have written that line.

I don't know that the lovely inhabitants of your beautiful city need any forewarnings, to make 'em avoid the breakers upon which our vessel was wrecked; but for fear they should some day shake their gory locks at me, I will make public a brief allusion to some of the painful circumstances which lately occurred in the eternal city.

Not many days ago the everlasting Yankees (may they live always when the devil gets 'em), made a valiant assault upon the city of the hills—the eternal city, where for a hundred years the Indian rivers have been blending their waters peacefully together—where the Choctaw children built their flutter mills, and toyed with frogs and tadpoles whilst these majestic streams were but little spring branches babbling along their sandy beds. For three days and nights our valiant troops had beat back the foul invader, and saved our pullets from their devouring jaws. For three days and nights we bade farewell to every fear, luxuriating upon the triumph of our arms, and the sweet juices of our strawberries and cream. For three days and nights fresh troops from the South poured into our streets with shouts that made the welkin ring, and the turkey bumps rise all over the flesh of our people. We felt that Rome was safe—secure against the assaults of the world, the flesh, and the devil, which last individual is supposed to be that horde of foul invaders who are seeking to flank us out of both bread and existence.

But alas for human hopes! Man that is born of woman (and there is no other sort that I know of) has but few days that is not full of trouble. Although the troops did shout, although their brass-band music swelled upon the gale, although the turkey bumps rose as the welkin rung, although the commanding general assured us that Rome was to be held at every hazard, and that on to-morrow the big battle was to be fought, and the foul invaders hurled all howling and bleeding to the shores of the Ohio, yet it transpired somehow that on Tuesday night the military evacuation of our city was peremptorily ordered. No note of warning—no whisper of alarm—no hint of the morrow came from the muzzled lips of him who had lifted our hopes so high. Calmly and coolly we smoked our killikinick, and surveyed the embarkation of troops, construing it to be some grand manœuvre of military strategy. About ten o'clock we retired to rest, to dream of to-morrow's victory. Sleep soon overpowered us like the fog that covered the earth, but nary bright dream had come, nary vision of freedom and glory. On the contrary, our rest was uneasy—strawberries and cream seemed to be holding secession motions within our corporate limits,

SKEDADDLE IN THE HIGHWAY. p. 87.

when suddenly, in the twinkling of an eye, a friend aroused us from our slumber and put a new phase upon the "situation." General Johnston was retreating, and the blue-nosed Yankees were to pollute our sacred soil the next morning. Then came the tug of war. With hot and feverish haste we started out in search of transportation, but nary transport could be had. Time-honored friendship, past favors shown, everlasting gratitude, numerous small and lovely children, Confederate currency, new issues, bank bills, black bottles, and all influences were urged and used to secure a corner in a car, but nary corner—too late—too late—the pressure for time was fearful and tremendous—the steady clock moved on—no Joshua about to lengthen out the night, no rolling stock, no steer, no mule. With reluctant and hasty steps, we prepared to make good our exit by that overland line which railroads do not control, nor A. Q. Ms impress.

With our families and a little clothing, we crossed the Etowah bridge about the break of day on Wednesday, the 17th of May, 1864—exactly a year and two weeks from the time when General Forrest marched in triumph through our streets. By and by the bright rays of the morning sun dispersed the heavy fog, which like a pall of death had overspread all nature. Then were exhibited to our afflicted gaze a highway crowded with wagons and teams, cattle and hogs, niggers and dogs, women and children, all moving in dishevelled haste to parts unknown. Mules were braying, cattle were lowing, hogs were squealing, sheep were blating, children were crying, wagoners were cursing, whips were popping, and horses stalling, but still the grand caravan moved on. Everybody was continually looking behind, and driving before—everybody wanted to know every thing, and nobody knew any thing. Ten thousand wild rumors filled the circumambiant air. The everlasting cavalry was there, and as they dashed to and fro, gave false alarms of the enemy being in hot pursuit.

About this most critical juncture of affairs, some philanthropic friend passed by with the welcome news that the bridge was burnt, and the danger all over. Then ceased the panic, then came the peaceful calm of heroes after the strife of war is over—then exclaimed Frank Ralls, my demoralized friend, "Thank the good Lord for that. Bill, let's return thanks and stop and rest—boys let me get out and lie down—I'm as humble as a dead nigger—I tell you the truth—I sung the long metre doxology as I crossed the Etowah bridge, and I expected to be a dead man in fifteen minutes. Be thankful, fellows, let's all be thankful —the bridge is burnt, and the river is three miles deep. Good sakes, do you reckon those Yankees can swim? Get up, boys—let's drive ahead and keep moving—I tell you there's no accounting for any thing with blue clothes on these days—ding'd if I ain't afraid of a blue-tailed fly."

With a most distressing flow of language, he continued his rhapsody of random remarks.

BIG JOHN MAKES HASTE SLOWLY. p. 88.

Then there was that trump of good fellows, *Big John*—as clever as he is fat, and as fat as old Falstaff—with in*defat*igable diligence he had secured, as a last resort, a one-horse steer spring wagon, with a low, flat body sitting on two rickety springs. Being mounted thereon, he was urging a more speedy locomotion by laying on to the carcass of the poor old steer with a thrash-pole some ten feet long. Having stopped at a house, he procured a two-inch auger, and boring a hole through the dashboard, pulled the steer's tail through and tied up the end in a knot. "My running gear is weak," said he, "but I don't intend to be stuck in the mud. If the body holds good, and the steer don't pull off his tail, why, Bill, I am safe." "My friend," said I, "will you please to inform me what port you are bound for, and when you expect to reach it?" "No port at all, Bill," said he, "I'm going dead straight to the big Stone Mountain. I am going to get on the top and roll rocks down upon all mankind. I now forewarn every living thing not to come there until this everlasting foolishness is over." He was then but three miles from town, and had been travelling the livelong night. Ah, my big friend, thought I, When wilt thou arrive at thy journey's end? In the language of Patrick Henry, Will it be the next week or the next year? Oh that I could write a poem, I would embalm thy honest face in epic verse. I can only drop to thy pleasant memory a passing random rhyme?

Farewell, Big John, farewell!
'Twas painful to my heart
To see thy chances of escape,
Was that old steer and cart.

Methinks I see thee now,
With axletrees all broke,
And wheels with nary hub at all,
And hubs with nary spoke.

But though the mud is deep,
Thy wits will never fail;
That faithful steer will take thee out,
If thou wilt hold his tail.

Mr. Editor, under such variegated scenes we reported progress, and in course of time arrived under the shadow of thy city's wings abounding in gratitude and joy.

With sweet and patient sadness, the tender hearts of our wives and daughters beat mournfully as we moved along. Often, alas wow often, was the tear seen swimming in the eye, and the lip quivering with emotion, as memory lingered around deserted homes, and thoughts dwelt upon past enjoyments and future desolation. We plucked the wild flowers as he passed, sang songs of merriment, exchanged our wit with children—smothering, by every means, the sorrow of our fate. These things, together with the comic events that occurred by the way, were the safety-valves that saved the poor heart from bursting. But for these, our heads would have been fountains and our hearts a river of tears. Oh, if some kind friend would set our retreat to music, it would be greatly appreciated indeed. It should be a plaintive tune, interspersed with occasional comic notes and frequent fuges scattered promiscuously along.

Our retreat was conducted in excellent good order, *after the bridge was burnt.* If there was any straggling at all, they straggled ahead. It would have delighted General Johnston to have seen the alacrity of our movements.

The great struggle of our contest seemed to be which army could retreat the fastest—General Johnston's or ours—which could outflank the other—and I allow as it was pull Dick, pull devil, between 'em. It is a source of regret, however, that some of our households of the African scent have fallen back into the arms of the foul invaders. I suppose they may now be called miscegenators, and by this time are increasing the stock of *Odour d'Afrique* in Northern society, which popular perfume crowds out of the market all those extracts which made X. Bazin Jules Haule and Lubin famous. Good-bye, sweet otto of roses; farewell, ye balm of a thousand flowers—your days are numbered.

But I must close this melancholy narrative, and hasten to subscribe myself

Your runagee,
BILL ARP.

P. S.—Tip is still faithful unto the end. He says the

old turkey we left behind has been setting for fourteen weeks, and the fowl invaders are welcome to *her*. Furthermore, that he threw a dead cat in the well, and they are welcome to that.

B. A.

TIP WELCOMES THE FOWL INVADER. p. 92.

HIS LATE TRIALS AND ADVENTURES.

Some frog-eating Frenchman has written a book, and called it "Lee's Miserables," or some other such name, which I suppose contains the misfortunes of poor refugees in the wake of the Virginny army. General Hood has also got a few miserables in the suburbs of his fighting-ground, and if any man given to romance would like a fit subject for a weeping narrative, we are now ready to furnish the mournful material.

As the Yankees remarked at Bull Run, "these are the times that try men's soles," and I suppose my interesting family is now prepared to show stone bruises and blisters with anybody. It is a long story, Mr. Editor, and cannot possibly be embraced in a single column of your wandering newspaper; but I will condense it as briefly as possible, smoothing over the most affecting parts so as not to occasion too great a diffusion of sympathetic tears.

After our hasty flight from the eternal city, we became

converted over to the doctrine of squatter sovereignty, and pitched our tents in the piney woods. Afar off in those fields of illimitable space, we roamed through the abstruse regions of the philosophic world. There no unfriendly soldier was perusing around and asking for papers. There the melancholy mind was soothed. There the lonely runnagee could contemplate the sandy roads, the wire-grass woods, and the million of majestic pines that stood like ten-pins in an alley, awaiting some huge cannon-ball to come along and knock 'em down. The mountain scenery in this romantic country was grand, gloomy, and peculiar, consisting in numberless gopher-hills, spewed up in promiscuous beauty as far as the eye could reach. All around us, the swamp frogs were warbling their musical notes. All above us, the pines were sighing and singing their mournful tunes. Dame Nature has spread herself there in showing her lavish hand, and wasting timber along those endless glades. Truly, we were treading on classic ground, for we pitched our tents in a blackberry patch, and morning, noon, and night, luxuriated in peace upon the delicious fruit which everywhere adorned the sandy earth.

But those piney woods to which we fled, did not, by any means, agree with our ideas of future comfort. After it had rained some forty days and forty nights without a recess, the corn crop had pretty well died out, and General Starvation seemed about to assume command of the regions round about. Our nearest neighbor cropped it over some seven hundred acres of scattering land, situated from six to ten inches under water. Taking a wade with him one day over his farm, we concluded that if it didn't rain any more and the entire crop was prudently gathered, he might probably make a peck to the acre of peckerwood nubbins. The hopes of the family seemed to fix upon the prospect of a pea crop that was yet to come, and it was sorrowfully amusing to see the old gentleman looking everywhere for an early blossom. He found one at last, and 'lighting from his mule, he sat on a lightwood stump close by for half an hour, and would have stayed longer, no doubt, if I hadn't induced him away. "Did you see any sign of peas?" said the good lady. "Yes, madam," said I. "How many do you think we will make?" said she. "I think, mam," said I, "if it stops raining, you may make some twenty-five or thirty."

"Alas, poor Yorik," as Sam Patch said. In a week more the army worm had come along and devoured every pea-vine upon the plantation. We felt constrained to depart from those coasts, and seek an Egypt somewhere in a rounder and more rolling country. Accordingly, we soon landed our interesting family at a depot on the Mobile and Girard Railroad, *en route* for Columbus. This little road is, in my opinion, the only respectable railway in the Confederate States. It is a small concern of its kind, it's true, for it don't run anywhere in particular, and only connects with a little spring branch in the piney woods, some forty-five miles from Columbus. When the branch goes dry, I suppose the train don't run quite so far, but stops at any pine-tree on the way after the last passenger gets off. The floor of the nice new passenger car is sprinkled all over every morning with clean white sand, and you can mix yourself up with the ladies like unto the olden time before the war, and the mumps, and the measles broke loose. No gray-eyed soldier stands on the platform to keep you out. No rusty bayonet is pointing about to make a man feel mean. No passport agent comes sliding along asking for papers. On the contrary, all is quiet and peaceful, and the kind-hearted conductor is only anxious to collect your fare, and make you comfortable.

All along the line, at every station, pretty women get on and off. When they leave us, an affectionate man like myself unconsciously whispers, "Depart in peace, ye treasures of delight." As the train moves off we cast a longing, lingering look behind, exclaiming in the beautiful language of Mr. Shakspeare, 'I have thee not, but yet I see thee still.' Farewell, sweet darlings, until I come again. Be careful, Mr. Coleman, of your precious freight, and when you tire of your delightful position, just tell Mr. Mitchell to consider me in. But woman is sometimes very variegated and peculiar in the way she does. I am just reminded how, on a late occasion, I found but one vacant seat in the car after I located my numerous and interesting family. A luxurious lady, with some aggravating

LUXURIANT LADY WITH AGGRAVATING CURLS. p. 97.

curls, had occupied nearly all of a seat, spreading herself like a setting-hen, all over the velvet cushion. "Madam, can I share this seat with you?" said I. "Certainly, sir," and she closed in her skirts some several inches. In a short space of time she became affected with drowsiness. Her neck became as limber as a greasy rag. Leaning on my shoulder, she seemed wonderfully affectionate, as her head kept bobbing around, and I felt very peculiar at such times as she would subside into my palpitating bosom. About this critical juncture, I ventured to turn my astonished gaze towards Mrs. Arp, and seeing that she was waiting for some remark, I observed, "Hadn't I better remove my seat? Do you think I can endure the like of this?"

"I do not, William," said she. "You had better stand up awhile, and when you get tired some of the children will relieve you." The glance of her eye and the manner in which she spoke brought me up standing, and gave me a correct view of the situation. Immediately I assumed a perpendicular attitude, and the curly head was left without a prop. I assure you, Mr. Editor, a man's wife is the best judge of such peculiar things; and as for me, I am always governed by it.

We arrived in Atlanta about the time the first big shells commenced scattering their unfeeling contents among the suburbs of that devoted city. Then come the big panics; then shrieked the man-eater; then howled the wild hyena among the hills of Babylon. All sorts of people seemed moving in all sorts of ways, with an accelerated motion. They gained ground on their shadows as they leaned forward on the run, and their legs grew longer at every step. With me it was the second ringing of the first bell. I had sorter got used to the thing, and set myself down to take observations. "How many miles to Milybright?" said I. But no response came, for their legs were as long as light, and every bursting shell was an old witch on the road. Cars was the all in all. Depots were the centre of space, converging lines from every point of the compass made tracks to the offices of railroad superintendents. These functionaries very prudently vamosed the ranche to avoid their too numerous friends, leaving positive orders to their subordinates. The passenger depot was thronged with anxious seekers of transportation. "Won't you let these boxes go as baggage?" "No, madam, it is impossible." Just then somebody's family trunk as big as a nitre bureau was shoved in, and the poor woman got desperate. "All I've got ain't as heavy as that," said she; "I am a poor widow, and my husband was killed in the army. I've got five children, and three of them cutting teeth, and my things have got to go." We took up her boxes and shoved them in. Another good woman asked very anxiously for the Macon train. "There it is, madam," said I. She shook her head mournfully and remarked, "You are mistaken, sir, don't you see the engine is headed right up the State road,

ATLANTA PANICS. p. 99.

towards the Yankees? I sha'n't take any train with the engine at that end of it. No, sir, that ain't the Macon train." Everywhere was hurrying to and fro at a lively tune. "What's to-day, nigger," said a female darkey, with a hoop skirt on her arm. "'Tain't no day, honey, dat eber I seed. Yestiday was Sunday, and I reckon to-day is Runday from de way de white folks are movin' about. Yah, yah; ain't afeered of Yankees myself, but dem sizzin bum-shells kill a nigger quicker dan you can lick your tongue out. Gwine to git away from here—I is."

I went into a doctor's shop, and found my friend packing up his vials and poisons and copaiva and such like. Various excited individuals come in, looked at a big map on the wall, and pointed out the roads to McDonough and Eatonton and Jasper, and soon their proposed lines of travel were easily and greasily visible from the impression of their perspiring fingers. An old skeleton, with but one leg, was swinging from the ceiling, looking like a mournful emblem of the fate of the troubled city. "You are going to leave him to stand guard, doctor?" said I. "I suppose I will," said he; "got no transportation for him." "Take the screw out of his skull," said I, "and give him a crutch, maybe he will travel; all flesh is moving and I think the bones will catch the contagion soon."

A few doors further, and a venerable auctioneer was surveying the rushing, running crowd, and every now and then he would raise his arm with a seesaw motion and exclaim, "Going—going—gone ! Who's the bidder ?" "Old Daddy Time," said I, "he'll get them all before long." The door of an old friend's residence swung open to my gaze, and I walked in. Various gentlemen of my acquaintance were discussing their evidences of propriety over a jug of departing spirits. "I believe I'll unpack," said one, "dinged if I'm afraid of a blue-tailed fly ; I'm going to sit down and be easy. "In a horn," said I. Just then a sizzing, singing, crazy shell sung a short-metre hymn right over the house. "Jake, has the dray come ?" he said, bouncing to his feet ; "confound that dray—blame my skin if I'll ever get a dray to move these things—boys, let's take another drink." After which, another friend remarked, "Boys, let's all stay ; durned if it don't look cowardly to run ! Boys, here's to—who shall we drink to ?" "Here's to Cassabianca," said I. "Good, good," they all shouted. "Here's to Cabysianka. Let me speak it for you, boys," said our host ; "I've spoken it a thousand times." He mounted the seat of a broken sofa, and spreading himself, declaimed :

"'The boy stood burning on the deck,
When all had fled but him.'"

"That's me," said one. "It's me exactly," said another. "I'm Cabysianka myself—dog my cat if I don't be the last one to leave this ship." Another shell sizzed, and bursted a few yards off. "Boys, let's take another drink and leave the town—dod rot the Yankees." "Here's to—here's to—the—the 'Last of the Mohikans'" said I. "Exactly—that's so. I'm him myself. I'm the mast of the Lohikens; durned if I'll leave these diggings as long as—as long as——" "As the State Road," said I, "which is now about four inches and a half." "That's it; that's so," said my friends. "Here's to the State Road and Dr. Brown and Joe Phillips, as long as four inches and a half."

By and by the shells fell as thick as Governor Brown's proclamations, causing a more speedy locomotion in the excited throng who hurried by the door, but my friends inside had passed the Rubicon, and one by one retired to dream of Botzaris and his Suliote band. Vacant rooms and long corridors echoed with their snores, and they appeared like sleeping heroes in the halls of the Montezumas.

In the blessed days gone by, I have seen the shaking Quakers going through their pious motions and peculiar attitudes. I have curiously watched and waited to discover the first shake of the spiritual leg. Then another and another would catch the delicious trembles, until the entire assembly of brethren and sisters were shuffling their extremities in solemn and hysteric beauty. Just so the big panics seemed to inspire the good people of Atlanta. The first good shake that occurred on Peachtree was a foul contagion that soon spread its awful trembles from the barracks to the fair grounds, sweeping in its all-gathering course the excited population who peopled its busy streets.

Eminent physicians have said that contagious diseases are catching. It is certain they are well calculated to bring mankind to a horizontal position, and prostrate the energies of both mind and body. But, from my own observation, the Atlanta big panics reverse the engine, and brings folks to an active perpendicular quicker than all the physic ever seen in a city drug-store. It certainly has a tendency to arouse the dormant energies of feeble invalids. Weak backs and lame legs, old chronics and rheumatics, in fact, all the internal diseases which honest fear of powder and ball had developed since the war began, were now forgotten in the general flight; and the examining boards could have seen many a discharge invalidated, and a *living, moving lie* given to their certificates.

All day and all night long the iron horses were snorting to the echoing breeze. Train after train of goods and chattels moved down the road, leaving hundreds of anxious faces waiting their return. There was no method in this madness. All kinds of plunder was tumbled in promiscuously. A huge parlor mirror, some 6 feet by 8, all bound in elegant gold, with a brass buzzard spreading his wings on the top, was set up at the end of the car and reflected a beautiful assortment of parlor furniture to match, such as pots, kettles, baskets, bags, barrels, kegs, bacon, and bedsteads piled up together. Government officials had the preference and Government officials all have friends. Any clever man with a charming wife or a pretty sister could secure a corner in more cars than one, and I will privately mention to you, Mr. Editor, that I have found a heap of civility on this account myself. Indeed, I have always thought that no man is excusable who has not either one or the other.

I now reluctantly proceed to that melancholy crisis which seemed to have a personal relation to my family. By the time that the city of Atlanta was somewhat purified of its population, I concluded that discretion was the better part of valor, and so prepared to transfer my interesting family to some convenient point on the Georgia Railroad. We took the train one morning without any definite idea where we would stop. "Tickets, sir," said the conductor. "Nary ticket," said I. "How far are you going?" said he. Putting on an air of sublime indifference, I remarked that "I was not very particular—that he knew the road and could suit himself." He cut his eye along the line of my numerous offspring, and observed that I had better scatter them, as provisions were scarce. I paid him our fare to Covington, and so got rid of his impertinence.

Here I found friends—dear friends, some of whom had tasted the bitterness of a running life, and were fully prepared to appreciate our situation. Confiding my family to their care, I journed to Lawrenceville in search of transportation. There I found to my dismay that every thing that moved on wheels and all four-footed beasts had been stampeded to a distant wilderness. I arranged it, however, that rolling stock should be procured from the Mulberry Hills and sent to Covington with all possible despatch. Confident of success, I took myself to a retired refuge which had been offered us, 'way up on the banks of the Chattahoochee, there to await the arrival of my family.

Day after day passed by, and night after night was specked with melancholy stars, but no family arrived, no rolling stock appeared coming over the distant hill. Rumors were rampant—aggravating rumors of a terrible raid. To relieve my suspense I became an infantry scout, and started in pursuit of knowledge under many difficulties. I had not travelled very far before I found to a moral certainty that I was cut off and blockaded, if not surrounded and ambuscaded. The everlasting Yankees were out on a raid—a devilish raid, an infernal raid. They were in Lawrenceville and had come from Covington, and according to reliable information, had stolen all the horses, burnt every dwelling, hung all the men, drowned all the children, and carried off the women alive. Frantic and furious, I rushed on all ready to fight, one against a thousand, and fate and destiny thrown in to boot. I cannot tell to this day how they heard I was coming, but certain it is, when I reached the village of Lawrenceville the raid had retired. I pre pared to pursue my journey, when I perceived a wandering son of Ethiopia coming down from the Covington road. Recognizing him, I inquired what he knew. "Dem Yankees been to Covington, sir." And what else? "Missus left 'em and went to de Circle, sir, and Tip went back atter de baggage, sir." And what else? Talk fast. "And dey got Tip's mules, sir." Go on. "And all de baggage, sir." Don't stop, boy. "And dey got Tip, sir; and dey made him dig his grave, sir; and dey went atter missus and de children, sir; and dey carried 'em all off, sir." "Stop, boy," said I, "let me sit down, I am dizzy—bring me some water." In a few minutes I rallied sufficiently to cross-examine this blubbering darkey, and found that my family had escaped from Covington, and went to Social Circle. All else was rumor and nigger talk.

About this time a messenger from the wilderness brought news that the rolling stock had been sent in due time, and nearly reached the journey's end, when the news of the raid caused a sudden reaction of course and motion. They hurried away by forced marches under cover of night and sought safety in the wilderness. Where, then, was my family, and how did they travel? Tip was there, and Tip was a host, I knew, but Tip couldn't make wagons nor mules, and there was none in the neighborhood that I could hear of. The baggage is gone, I suppose, said I—all gone. The big trunk and little trunk, and bonnet trunk, and the boys' trunk, and the girls' trunk, and the general trunk—all gone. A thousand garments more or less, for there was dresses, frocks, shawls, collars, caps, furs, flannels, skirts with hoops and without, shoes, stockings, aprons, gloves, handkerchiefs, breeches, drawers, coats, jackets, cloaks, bonnets, and all the mysterious garments which are worn out of sight—all gone. And this was all we saved of a once happy home. Ah! that Mr. Shakspeare were here to immortalize the sorrow of our melancholy fate. I don't mind trouble when it comes but once in a while; but twice in a while, or three times in a while, is crushing my energies.

While brooding over these imaginary evils, a welcome voice broke its familiar sounds upon my ear. Looking up, my delighted vision perceived the immortal and heroic Tip. I knew he had good news, for he always brings it. He never waited for interrogatories, but announced, "Mas William, all safe in Madison—every thing safe—nary loss on our side—glorious victory."

Reader, dear reader, I revived. It cannot be recorded how good a man can feel away in the recesses of his heart. With a voice all serene I asked: "Is my entire family all safe, Tip, my boy?" "Every one, sir," said he; "I counted 'em when I got to Madison, and I counted 'em agin when I left 'em, sir. All safe, sir—baby and all—and de big trunk, and de little trunk, and de bonnet trunk, and de boys' trunk, and de girls' trunk, and de genrell trunk."

The faithful Tip then informed me how they waited for

my return, and how the Yankees did come on a raid, and cavorted about, and how the ladies let down all the valuables in the well except the baby, and like to hid that in the same subterranean hole, and how finally a friend from Madison came to the rescue, and stole them all off by night; and how my friend had sent him all away round by Athens and Jefferson in search of a lost man by the name of Arp. "That's me," said I, "I'm him, myself. I will rest to-night, and grease my blisters; to-morrow we will take it afoot to the wilderness, and procure transportation once more." On this journey every thing worked well, and I reached the bosom of my family on Sunday night. Then all went merry as a marriage bell until breakfast-time next morning, when it was hurriedly announced that the Yankees were in town on a raid. The unsatisfied, ubiquitous, infernal wretches! THREE TIMES. "THRICE THE BRINDLE CAT HATH MEWED."

Our friends lived in the suburbs, and we thereby got a little time for action. In a few minutes we limbered to the rear, and from a retired eminence overlooked the enemy's operations. My family had by this time become somewhat acclimated to their poisonous presence, and so between the house and the woods we established an African telegraph to communicate the enemy's progress. But the enemy made no demonstration towards our end of the town.

They soon retreated for parts unknown, without doing material damage, except in the way of stealing and plundering for jewelry and horses. I had before this converted my wife's piano into salt, and the salt was packed up in the depot at Madison, waiting for transportation. The raid didn't burn it, but I will mention right here, that not long after this narrow escape, a kind-hearted man by the name of Sherman came along with a parcel of blue devils and put a torch to the depot, and my salt wasn't salty enough to save itself. By no means. It went up a spout. I had never told Mrs. Arp that I had sold her piano and put the money in salt. She thinks to this day that it was her piano that was burnt, and I hope she will never find out to the contrary, for I'd rather she'd flash the fire in those eyes at the Yankees than at me.

After a week of delightful recreation—a week of unalloyed enjoyment in the society of pleasant friends, we once more began our journey to the banks of the Chattahoochee.

We had anticipated much comfort and satisfaction in getting off the line of railroads and travelling overland to our destination. Railroads don't suit a runnagee like an old-fashioned dirt road. They are so liable to be raided, invaded, and blockaded, and ambuscaded, and enfiladed, and the great trouble is, they don't fork enough. Ever since this everlasting war, I have been partial to a forked dirt road, for it gives a poor runnagee choice of direction every few miles. It's so easy to stop or go on, or dodge in the woods, and change latitude and longitude.

It was refreshing to stop by the wayside and answer the inquiries about the great war, and the artillery, and hear them tell over the horses and mules that Gen. Wheeler's cavalry had come along and stolen in their neighborhood.

At last we found an end to our trials and tribulations, for a time at least. We run the gauntlet of Yankee raids and rebel cavalry, looking upon the latter as did Ali Baba upon the forty thieves, and dreading the former as the devil let loose for a thousand years. Betwixt the one and the other a poor runnagee had as well be among the Turks and wild Arabs of the African desert. How we escaped this combination of evils I know not, except it be that the writ of habeas corpus, restored to us by our Governor and his friends, operated like an unseen and mystic shield to protect us on the way.

We have now tried Mr. Sherman's front and his flanks, and found no peace; for the future we shall rest in the rear of his army, until dislodged by causes unknown and unforeseen. We cannot run again, for the reason urged by the Texan, who, when he got into trouble, took counsel of a lawyer as to what he should do. His case was so bad that the faithful attorney advised him to run away. "The devil," says he, "where shall I run to? I'm in Texas now."

Yours truly,

BILL ARP.

BILL ARP TO THE REBEL.

Rome, Ga., *December* 28, 1864.

Dear Rebel: After suffering all the trials and tribulations of which St. Paul makes mention in his Epistle to the Corinthians (xi. chap., 24 to 30th ver.), I have once more reached my home in the city of the hills. "Desolation was wrecked upon this coast," and my own beautiful home has groaned under the weight of a merciless oppression.

Could you stand upon the hills of this desolate city and see its wasted and withered beauties—could you traverse our cemetery hill, that once so beautifully hung its clustered shades over the banks of our rivers, I know you would feel that there was no fitness in a union with that people. The wanton destruction of all those ornaments with which we had adorned the homes of our dead, has murdered our Christian charity and stabbed our forgiveness to the quick. The digging of rifle-pits through the cemetery might possibly have been a military necessity, but it was a brutal insult to our dead to undermine their graves.

Their harmless bones might have been removed to some quiet spot. It was intensely fiendish to take our ornaments and tombstones and place them like rock and rubbish in their fortifications—to shatter the iron railing into a thousand fragments—to pitch their tents right over the ground where our loved ones were resting in hallowed peace—to beat their tattoo and reveille, and sing their rude songs, and chuckle their devilish merriment right over the homes of our dead—the sacred spots where we had planted the fairest flowers to sweeten their sad graves. In taking a survey of this desolate and desecrated place, I have thought that if the spirits of the dead did love to linger around their graves, they must have wandered far away from this tumultuous and unquiet ground.

Within the same enclosure there rests in peace some seven hundred of our enemies' dead, their graves in long rows of marked precision, every one carefully hilled, and having neat painted head-boards with name, and rank, and company, and regiment. No Southern Vandal has yet been found to disturb or displace a single clod. There I trust they will rest in unmolested quiet, as a contrast to the brutal meanness of the Yankee nation. Nevertheless, we are but too happy to return; and should the heartless, pitiless invaders of our peace disturb us here no more, we will soon restore many of the charms that clustered around our doors.

How feelingly and forcibly would I repeat the language of Mr. Davis to the Northern people—"Let us alone!"

> "Oh, for one short year,
> To feel as I used to feel!"

I am tired of living an exile's life, for I have been a most unlucky "runnagee." Three times was my family overtaken by the abominable raiders.

> "Thrice the brindle cat hath mewed,
> Thrice and once the hedge-pig whined."

Oh that we could now say, "Never more a refugee!" Job was a good man and suffered much—very much. He stood the test of all the severe afflictions his Maker visited upon him; but from a careful examination of his sacred record, I do not find that he was ever a refugee. Should this test have been applied, I am not prepared to say that he would have stood up to his integrity.

The wanderers are returning daily, and it would do your persecuted soul good to see us shake hands with them as they come. The Lord has been merciful unto us and blessed us in one thing. He has purged our population of its scum—most of the tories and vagabonds went off with the Yankees, and our only regret is that *one more train* did not come. There were a few more who got ready to go, but could not for want of transportation. They are still here. It gives us the heartburn to look at them.

But I only started to write for your paper to be sent to my address at this place. We must have the news. We know nothing about our army that is reliable—hear a rumor that Sherman has reached the coast in safety. Well, if he has, we can *now* see a thousand ways how he could have been demolished. It reminds me of the fellow who put up a shanty in the suburbs of Augusta, wherein to sell truck, and trade on a small scale. A customer called in and asked if he had any onions for sale. "None, sir," said the huckster. After the customer had got off about a hundred yards, the trader woke up from a spell of thinkin' and exclaimed: "I wonder if that dam fool could have meant *inguns*." Of which latter article he had plenty. Now, if we had only known that Sherman meant *inguns*, how easily we could have sold him!

BILL ARP PHILOSOPHIZES UPON THE WAR, Etc.

Mr. Editor—

Sir: If I could discern any thing gloomy in the political horizon, I would keep it to myself, and not go to putting my long face in the newspapers; but seeing things as I see 'em, I don't see any thing in the situation more distressing than usual.

My doctrine has always been, that if we was to fight and fight and fight until our army was played out, the biggest part of old Lincoln's job would be just begun. After he has whipped us, then he has got to subjugate us. He has got to hold us down, and he can't do it. I used to have a neighbor who was one of these mean, little, snarling, fic-dog sort of men, and I had him to whip about once a week for three months, but I didn't make a thing off of him. He would raise a new fuss with me in an hour after I had made him holler enough, and finally I sold him my land, and moved away just to get rid of him. Now the idea of old Lincoln taking possession of so many towns and cities, and so much territory, and holding it and keeping so many people down, is utter nonsense, and it can't be done. Besides, we are not whipped yet—not by three or four jug fulls. Suppose Sherman did walk right through the State. Suppose he did. Was anybody whipped? Didn't the rebellion just close right up on the ground behind him, just like shutting up a pair of waffle-irons? He parted the atmosphere as he went along, and it collapsed again in his rear immediately. He will have to go over that old ground several times yet, and then sell out and move away.

Well, they say that old Abe's Congress has finally and forever set free all the niggers, by amending the Constitution. How did that free 'em, or how did freeing 'em amend the Constitution? The darned old thing has been broke for forty years, and it is broke yet; but suppose they have freed 'em, it is no more than old Abe has done three or four times by his proclamations. What does it all amount to?—I want to buy a nigger, and I had just as lief by a chunk of a *free* nigger as any other sort. I don't care a bobee about his being free, if I can subjugate him; and if he gets above his color, I will put thirty-nine whelks right under his shirt, and make him wish that old Lincoln stood in his shoes.

But, Mr. Editor, Sir: The way I see it is, that if we are to be whipped at all, then the infantry, which is to say the web-feet, are to be whipped first. After that, then comes the tug of war. Whipping the cavalry will be the devilishest undertaking of this or any preceding conflict. I tell you, sir, they can't be whipped until they are caught, and that event will never transpire. The truth is, that the Confederate cavalry can fight 'em, and dog 'em, and dodge 'em, and bushwhack 'em, and bedevil 'em, for a thousand years, and that is as long as the most sanguine have calculated this war to last. The Confederate cavalry are ubiquitous and everlasting. I have travelled a heap of late, and had occasion to retire into some very sequestered regions, but nary hill or holler, nary vale or valley, nary mountain gorge or inaccessible ravine have I found, but what the cavalry had been there, and *just left.* And that is the reason they can't be whipped, for they have always *just left*, and took an odd horse or two with 'em. For four years the Confederate Horse-Stealing Cavalry have been pirooting around, preparing themselves for the frightful struggle that is to come. By dodging around they have completed their inspection of stock, and tried all its bottom, and now it is reasonable to suppose they are ready to fight. The fact is, Mr. Editor, stealing from our side is most played out, and I feel assured our enemies will suffer very soon. Such a crisis is, I reckon, a blessing to the country, for when we have lost all of our property, there won't be nothing to reconstruct, and we will all go to fighting. Property in such a time is the bane of liberty. Old Blivins remarked, that if we all had been as poor as him when the war begun, and had held our own, the victory would have been won long ago. "How poor are you, Blivins?" said I. "Just four years ago," said he, "I was even with the world, which is to say I owed about as many as I didn't owe, and had nothing to boot, and that is the fix I want the Confederacy to get in."

We are that way in these parts, Mr. Editor, sure. What the Yankees didn't get in six months' continuous plunder, was brought out to enjoy when they left. Suddenly some friendly scouts appeared upon the arena, and made a general grab. Every thing visible was appropriated without pay or ceremony. Our indignant citizens appealed for protection, and his Excellency the Governor sent up a major as the avenger of our wrongs, and the protector of our lives and property. The Major and his gallant boys appreciated our cause, and in order to prevent a recurrence of such robberies by the wandering scouts, they stole all the balance themselves and then run away. Such is war, Mr. Editor, but nevertheless, notwithstanding, I am for it as long as possible, and longer if necessary.

We are now trying the militia—the Georgia militia—luxuriating under their benign and peaceable rule. Slandered as they have been from the mountain to the sea, they are now the guardians of our sleeping liberties. Like a wall of fire they environ the outposts of Cherokee Georgia, and we will stand by 'em as long as—they stand by us. Let their slanderers beware, and recollect the fate of Ike

Johnson, that old veteran from the Virginia army. Ike was at home on a busting furlow, and he rode up to the militia and pulling out his repeater, exclaimed, with uncommon gravity, "*Lay down, meelish, I am going to bust this cap.* Mr Editor, Ike Johnson had to leave those parts prematurely.

And now, sir, will you allow us Romans to ask a favor of your wide-spreading paper? We desire you to intersperse in your columns some news of the Georgia Legislature. We understood they were powerfully scattered, and somewhat demoralized. Have they rallied yet, and did the Governor lose many of the public archives? I saw a member from Franklin the other day, and he had two pair of cotton cards in his hand. I asked him about the archives, and he said he understood the Governor got off about ten thousand pair of 'em, and that all the members got two pair apiece besides.

Do you suppose this is so?

Yours politely,

BILL ARP.

BILL ARP ON THE CURRENCY.

Mr. Editor—

Sir: At this time I am not as much in favor of soft money as I was. I don't want to raise no rumpus nor hurt nobody's feelings, but somehow I am induced from peculiar circumstances to express my opinion about the way my finances have been managed by other people.

Mr. Trenholm, I suppose, is a mighty smart man, and knows how to run the money machine, but surely he don't know how the last currency bill affects me and my neighbors. I don't know much about banking nor financiering, nor the like of that, but I can't be honeyfuggled as to how my money comes and how it goes. I know how proud I was of the first Confederate bill that crossed the feel of my fingers. How carefully I put it low down in my breeches pocket, and kept my hand on it all the way home! I felt proud because the Confederacy owed me. Thinks, says I to myself, this is a big thing certain, and I will invest my bottom dollar in this kind of money, and lay it away for hard times.

Well, after while, Mr. Memminger, or Congress, or somebody, got up a bill, the substance of which were about as follows: "Mr. Arp, Sir: I bought some supplies from you for my army, and I give you my notes. Now if you will consolidate 'em and wait twenty years for the money, I will pay you four per cent. interest. If you won't do it, I will repudiate one-third of the debt, and won't take any of it for what you owe me for taxes." Mr. Editor, it didn't take *two* to make that bargain—it only took one. I hurried off to the agency, and consolidated. They took my money and give me a little sickly scrap of yellow printing, about the size of a thum paper, and I kept it and kept it, until I was obliged to have some change, and I sold it to a white man for fifty cents in the dollar. I took my pay in a parcel of hundred-dollar bills, drawing interest at two cents a day, and having a picture of an engine pulling a train of cars right under a telegraph wire, and the steam a-biling out all over it. Thinks, says I to myself, this here is a big thing certain and sure, for it is the right size, and it is drawing interest, and it is good for taxes during the war, for it says so on the upper left hand-corner.

Now, Mr. Trenholm, N. B., take notice. You come into office, then you or Congress or somebody fixed up a bill, which says in substance: "Oh, see here, Mr. Arp. We forgot about them interest notes when we made you fund your other money. You must come up in a few days and fund them too. If you don't you can't keep 'em, and we won't pay you any more intrest after the 1st of January, 1865, and we will tax 'em five per cent, and we won't take 'em for any thing you owe us." Well I concluded to hold 'em, interest or no interest, tax or no tax, for I have got to spend them very soon and they are more convenient than thum papers. I put 'em on the market, and the very best offer I could get was fifty cents on the dollar, and the interest thrown in. I thought that the merchants had combined to swindle me, but I got hold of a paper containing your last big currency bill, and its language to me is in substance as follows: "Mr. Arp, sir, since the 17th day of February, 1864, we have borrowed a heap of money, and give our notes, called the *new issue.* Now we want to make the holders come up and fund these notes, and we are going to mortgage corn and cotton enough to secure 'em. As for them interest bills of yours we can't do any thing for 'em—the fact is, we have left them out in the cold. It will take all the cotton and corn to secure the new issue. Oh, see here, Mr. Arp, you will have to bring over your cotton and grain to help us out, for we are bound to have it. Good, morning, sir."

That is it exactly, Mr. Trenholm. That is the way it works me and my neighbors. We can't help ourselves, but is a hurting us, way down in our bosoms. I had six hundred dollars of the old issue, and I promised Mrs. Arp some of it to buy her a cow. The funding business reduced it to three hundred dollars in them interest notes.

Your currency bill has put them down to one hundred and fifty, and it won't buy the hide and tallow of flatwoods heifer. I never hear my offspring crying for milk, but what I think of you affectionately, and exclaim—"Hard, hard indeed is the contest for freedom and the struggle for liberty," and I have also thought at such times, that if a man, a living man had treated me that way, if I couldn't whip him I would sue him in the big courts and the little courts and all other courts. I would cover him all over with warrants and summons, and subpœnas and interrogatories. He could get into jail for swindling just as easy as the captain of the forty thieves got into the robbers' cave.

Then, again, I get over it, and conclude that it couldn't be helped; but my deliberate opinion is, that it is just as easy for a Government to be honest as it is for a man, and is a heap more important. If Mr. Trenholm thinks so, he will buy Mrs. Arp a cow, and show his faith by his works. In the language of Mr. Milton, I don't want nothing but what is right.

Yours truly,

BILL ARP.

SHERMAN'S SENTINELS.

p. 123.

BILL ARP RETURNS TO THE ETERNAL CITY AND MEETS HIS FRIEND BIG JOHN.

MR. EDITOR—

Sir: I have not up to this time made any remarks in public about the trials and tribulations, the losses and crosses, the buzzards and dead horses seen on our journey to the eternal city. I shall not allude to it now, only to remark that our coming back was not so hasty as our leaving. It was in the dead of winter, through snow and through sleet, over creeks without bridges and bridges without floors, through a deserted and desolate land where no rooster was left to crow, no pig to squeal, no dog to bark, where the ruins of happy homes adorned the way, and ghostly chimneys stöod up like Sherman's sentinels a-guarding the ruins he had made. A little one-horse concern containing the highth of my worldly possessions, consisting of my numerous and lovely wife and children, and a shuck basket full of some second-class vittels. Counting our offspring, there was about ten of us in and about and around that wagon, thus illustrating what the poet has said, "One glorious hour of crowded life is worth an age without a name," though the glory was hard to pursue on such occasions. Mrs. Arp is of the opinion that her posterity was never as hungry before in their life as on that distressing journey, and she once remarked that there wasn't nary rod of the road that didn't hear some of 'em a-hollerin for vittels. My wife's husband is troubled because they ain't broke of it yet, and it does seem that the poorer I git the more devouring they bekum, all which will end in sumthing or other if sumthing don't happen.

We finally arrived within the precincts of our lovely home. The doors creaked welcome on their hinges, the hoppin-bug chirruped on the hearth, and the whistling wind was singing the same old tune around the bedroom corner. We were about as happy as we had been miserable, and when I remarked that General Vandiver, who occupied our house, must be a gentleman for not burning it, Mrs. Arp replied—

"I wonder what he done with my sewing machine."

"He didn't cut down our shade-trees," said I.

"My bureaus and carpets and crockery are all gone," said she.

"It may be possible," said I, "that the General——"

"And my barrel of soap," said she.

"It may be possible," said I, "that the General moved

off our things to take care of 'em for us. I reckon we'll get 'em all back after while."

"*After while*," said Mrs. Arp like an echo, and ever since then when I allude to our Northern brethren, she only replies, "*After while*."

By and by the scattered wanderers begun to drop in under the welcome shades of our sorrowful city. It was a delightful enjoyment to greet 'em home, and listen to the history of their sufferings and misfortunes. Misery loves company, and after the misery is past there's a power of comfort in talking it over and fixing up as big a tale as anybody. I was standing one day upon the banks of the Injun river, a-wonderin in my mind who would come next to gladden our hearts, when I saw the shadow of an object a-darkening the sunlit bank. It was not a load of hay or an elephant, but shore enough it was my friend Big John, a-movin slowly, but surely, to the dug-out landing on the opposite side. His big round face assumed more latitude when he saw me, and without waitin for remarks he sung out in a voice some two staves deeper than the Southern harmony—

"There came to the beech a *poor* exile of Erin!"

"Call him *fat*," said I, "and you'll fill the bill." Prouder to see him than a monkey show, I paddled the dug-out over in double quick and bid him welcum in the name of the eternal city and its humble inhabitants. I soon got him afloat in the little canoe, and before I was aware of it the water was sloshin over the gunnels at every wabble. "Lay down, my friend," said I, and he laid, which was all that saved us from a watery grave, and the neighborin farms from inundation. When safely landed I found him wedged in so tight that he couldn't rise, so I relieved him by a prize with the end of the paddle. As his foot touched the sacred soil he gently separated his countenance, and sung with feeling melody:

"Home again—home again—from a furrin shore,
The Yanks may com and the devil too, but I'll not run any more."

Recollectin some scraps of blank verse myself, I said with much accent, "Tell me thou swift of foot—thou modern Asahel—oh tell me where is thy chariot and steer? Where didst thou go when I did see thee driving like Jehu as we did flee for life?"

"I'll tell you all," sed he, "I want my friends to know it. I'm now a man of war, Bill, and I'm glad of it. I've done the State some service, and she knows it. I've handled guns—yes, guns—weapins of death. I've slept on my arms since I seen you—night after night have I slept on my arms, with hundreds of deadly weapins all around me. Ah, Bill, patriotism is a big thing. When you once break the ice, great sluices of glory as big as your arm will jest spring up like mushrooms in your bosom; and make you feel like throwing yourself clean away for your country. Let me sit down and I'll tell you all I know, Bill; but as the feller said in the theater, "when you in your letters these unlucky deeds relate, speak of me as I am—nothing expatiate nor set down hot in malice."

"Jest so," said I. "Proceed, my hero."

"Well, you see the night after you passed me, my steer got away. Hang the decievin beast! I hunted smartly for him the next mornin, but I hunted more forrerds than backwards. Leavin my wagin with a widder woman, I took it afoot across the country by a settlement road they called the 'cut-off.' Devil of a cut-off it was to me. I broke down in sight of a little log cabin, and never moved a foot further that day. The old man had a chunk of a nag that worked in a slide. I perswaded him to haul me to the end of the cut-off, and I know he done it for fear I'd eat up his smoke-house. Every now and then he'd look at the old 'oman, and she'd look at the smoke-house, and then look at me. But that slidin business were the most orfullest travellin that I ever hav had. Every time the pony'd look back he'd stop, and when he'd start agin he giv such a jerk that my contents were in danger. My holt broke on one okkashun, a-goin down a hill full of gullies. I rolled some twenty feet into the edge of the woods, and cotch up agin an old pine stump that was full of yaller jakets. Three of the dingd things stung me before I could rise, but I got through the cut-off and fell in with some empty wagons that was stampedin my way.

"Gittin on to Atlanta, a fool Irishman stopd me right at the edge of the town and demanded my papers. I didn't have no papers. Nobody had ever axd me for papers, but he wouldn't hear an argument. As Quarles would say, he wouldn't *jine issue*, but marched me to an office, and I didn't stay there ten minets. I was sent off to Decatur with some fifty conscripts, who wer all in mournin, exceptin their clothes. I never seed sich a pitiful set in my life. I talked with 'em all, and thar was nary one but what had the dyspepsy or the swinny, or the rumatics, or the blind staggers, or the heaves, or the humps, or sumthin. Well, there want none of us discharged, for there was bran new orders callin for everybody for thirty days to go to the ditches. As I couldn't walk that fur, I was ordered to Andersonville to guard the prisoners. At Macon I met an old acwaintance, who was a powerful big officer, and he had me transferred to his department, and put me in charge of his ordnance. There's where I handled guns, Bill, and slept on my arms. Whole boxes of muskets was around me, and I didn't no more mind taking a snooze on a gun box than if it had been a couch of fethery down. It's all in gittin use to it, Bill—all in the use."

"Jest so," said I, "that's the way I see it—exakly so, my friend, proceed."

"It's blamed lucky, Bill, that I didn't go to Andersonville. They would have had me alongside of Wirtz, either as principal or witness, or sumthin, and some lyin

BIG JOHN SLEEPS ON HIS ARMS. p. 128.

Yank would hav had a swear or two at me about shootin him on the dead line. Before this my carcass would hav been eat up by worms or cut up by doctors, and my picter spread all over a whole side of 'Harper's Weekly,' as a monster of deth.

"Well, I kept handlin guns and bayonets and dangerous weapons, until one day I got a furlo to go to Rome. Sherman was playin base around about Atlanta, and so I had to circumference around by the way of Selma, and the very day I got there, everlastin blast 'em, the Wilson raiders got there too. I wasn't no more lookin for them Yankees in Selma than I wer for old Belzebub, and both of 'em was all the same to me. Blamd if they wasn't shootin at me before I knowd they was in the State. How in the dickens they missed me I don't know, for their minny balls sung Yankee doodle all around me, and over me, and under me, and betwixt me.

"I tell you, Bill, I run like a mud turkel, lookin ahead of me at every step to find an easy place to fall when I was plugged. An old woman overtook me, and I axd her to take my watch and my money. She took 'em in a hurry and put 'em in her bosom. Well, I found a gully at last, and I rolld in kersplosh, for it was about two feet in mud and water. The infernals found me there jest at night, and got me out at the pint of the bayonet. They marched me to the wolf pen and there I stayd till the fuss was over.

"Right here, Bill, I want to make an observation.

There was a feller with me when I was cotch'd, and I seen him make a sorter of a sign to the captain, and they turned him loose in two minets, and he jest went anywhere as nateral as a king, while I had a crossey'd Dutchman standin over me with a bayonet grinnin from mornin till night. There was some Free Masonry about that, Bill, and if another one of these fool wars come along, I'll jine 'em if they'l let me.

"But I am at home now for good—I'm gwine to stay here like a sine die. I'm agin all wars and fightins. I'm opposed to all rows, and rumpusses, and riots. I don't keer nigh as much about a dog-fight as I used to. Now, if one could always see the end of a thing in advance, *and the end was all right*, I wouldn't mind a big fuss, but then you know a man's foresight ain't as good as his hind sights. If they was, this war wouldn't have broke out, and I wouldn't have lost my steer and my watch. I never seen that woman before nor since, and I wouldn't know her from any other woman that walks the earth—blam'd if I'm certain whether she was white or black. Bill, now is your offspring?"

"Hungry as usual, I thank you my friend," I said.

"How's Mrs. Arp?"

"Rebellious, John, very; but I think she'll be harmonized—*after while—after while.*"

Mr. Editor, I will not relate further of these trying adventures at this time. Big John is now entirely harmonious, and I suppose his future career will be all sereen.

Yours as ever,

BILL ARP.

P. S.—Mrs. Arp wants you to get back the letters I writ her when she was "sweet sixteen." Them officers have got 'em, and I suppose have laughed all the funny part away by this time. They contained some fool things that boys will write when they fall in love, and my wife sometimes used 'em upon me as reminders of broken promises.

She says if they'l send 'em, she'l try and forgive 'em—*after while.*

Don't trouble yourself *much*, Mr. Editor, and it will be all the same to me.

B. A.

BILL ARP ADDRESSES ARTEMUS WARD.

ROME, GA., *September* 1, 1865.

MR. ARTEMUS WARD, *Showman*—

SIR: The reason I write to you in perticler, is becaus you are about the only man I know in all "God's country" *so-called.* For some several weeks I hav been wantin to say sumthin. For some several years we rebs, *so-called,* but now late of said county deceased, have been tryin mighty hard to do somethin. We didn't quite do it, and now it's very painful, I assure you, to dry up all of a sudden, and make out like we wasn't there.

My friend, I want to say somethin. I suppose there is no law agin thinkin, but thinkin don't help me. It don't let down my thermometer. I must explode myself generally so as to feel better. You see I'm tryin to harmonize. I'm tryin to soften down my feelin's. I'm endeavoring to subjugate myself to the level of surroundin circumstances, *so-called.* But I can't do it until I am allowed to say somethin. I want to quarrel with sombody and then make friends. I ain't no giant-killer. I ain't no Norwegian bar. I ain't no boar-constrikter, but I'll be hornswaggled if the talkin and the writin and the slanderin has got to be all done on one side any longer. Sum of your folks have got to dry up or turn our folks loose. It's a blamed outrage, *so-called.* Ain't your editors got nothin else to do but to peck at us, and squib at us, and crow over us? Is every man what kan write a paragraph to consider us as bars in a cage, and be always a-jabbin at us to hear us growl? Now you see, my friend, that's what's disharmonious, and do you jest tell 'em, one and all, e pluribus unum, *so-called*, that if they don't stop it at once or turn us loose to say what we please, why we rebs, *so-called*, have unanimously and jointly and severally resolved to—to—to —think very hard of it—if not harder.

That's the way to talk it. I ain't agoin to commit myself. I know when to put on the brakes. I ain't agoin to say *all* I think, like Mr. Etheridge, or *Mr. Adderrig, so-called.* Nary time. No, sir. But I'll jest tell you, Artemus, and you may tell it to your show: If we ain't allowd to express our sentiments, we can take it out in *hatin;* and hatin runs heavy in my family, shure. I hated a man so bad once that all the hair cum off my head, and the man drownd himself in a hog-waller that night. I could do it agin, but you see I'm tryin to harmonize, to acquiesce, to becum calm and sereen.

Now I suppose that, poetically speakin,

"In Dixie's fall,
We sinned all."

But talkin the way I see it, a big feller and a little feller, *so-called*, got into a fite, and they fout and fout and fout a long time, and everybody all round kep hollerin hands off, but kep helpin the big feller, until finally the little feller caved in and hollered enuf. He made a bully fite I tell you, Selah. Well, what did the big feller do? Take him by the hand and help him up, and brush the dirt off his clothes? Nary time! No, sur! But he kicked him arter he was down, and throwd mud on him, and drug him about and rubbed sand in his eyes, and now he's gwine about hunting up his poor little property. Wants to confiscate it, *so-called*. Blame my jacket if it ain't enuf to make your head swim.

But *I'm* a good Union man, *so-called*. *I* ain't agwine to fight no more. *I* shan't vote for the next war. *I* ain't no gurilla. I've done tuk the oath, and I'm gwine to keep it, but as for my being subjugated, and humilyated, and amalgamated, and enervated, as Mr. Chase says, it ain't so —nary time. I ain't ashamed of nuthin neither—ain't repentin—ain't axin for no one-horse, short-winded pardon. Nobody needn't be playin priest around me. I ain't got no twenty thousand dollars. Wish I had; I'd give it to these poor widders and orfins. I'd fatten my own numerous and interestin offspring in about two minits and a half. They shouldn't eat roots and drink branch-water no longer. Poor, unfortunate things! to cum into this subloonary world at sich a time. There's four or five of 'em that never saw a sirkis nor a monky-show—never had a pocket-knife, nor a piece of cheese, nor a reesin. There's Bull Run Arp, and Harper's Ferry Arp, and Chikahominy Arp, that never saw the pikters in a spellin book. I tell you, my friend, we are the poorest people on the face of the earth—but we are poor and proud. We made a bully fite, Selah, and the whole American nation ought to feel proud of it. It shows what Americans can do when they think they are imposed on—"*so-called.*" Didn't our four fathers fight, bleed, and die about a little tax on tea, when not one in a thousand drunk it? Bekaus they succeeded, wasn't it glory? But if they hadn't, I suppose it would have been treason, and they would have been bowin and scrapin round King George for pardon. So it goes, Artemus, and to my mind, if the whole thing was stewed down it would make about a half pint of humbug. We had good men, great men, Christian men, who thought we was right, and many of 'em have gone to the undiscovered country, and have got a pardon as is a pardon. When I die I am mighty willing to risk myself under the shadow of their wings, whether the climate be hot or cold. So mote it be. Selah!

Well, maybe I've said enough. But I don't feel easy

yet. I'm a good Union man, certain and sure. I've had my breeches died *blue*, and I've bot a *blue* bucket, and I very often feel *blue*, and about twice in a while I go to the doggery and git *blue*, and then I look up at the *blue* serulean heavens and sing the melancholy chorus of the *Blue*-tailed Fly. I'm doin my durndest to harmonize, and think I could sucseed if it wasn't for sum things. When I see a black-guard goin around the streets with a gun on his shoulder, why right then, for a few minutes, I hate the whole Yanky nation. Jerusalem! how my blood biles! The institution what was handed down to us by the heavenly kingdom of Massachusetts, now put over us with powder and ball! Harmonize the devil! Ain't we human beings? Ain't we got eyes and ears and feelin and thinkin? Why, the whole of Africa has come to town, women and children and babies and baboons and all. A man can tell how fur it is to the city by the smell better than the mile-post. They won't work for us, and they won't work for themselves, and they'll perish to death this winter as shure as the devil is a hog, *so-called.* They are now basking in the summer's sun, livin on roasting ears and freedom, with nary idee that the winter will come agin, or that castor-oil and salts costs money. Sum of 'em, a hundred years old, are whining around about goin to kawlidge. The truth is, my friend, sombody's badly fooled about this bizness. Sombody has drawd the elefant in the lottery, and don't know what to do with him. He's jest throwing his snout

STUMP-TAIL DOG. p. 137.

loose, and by and by he'll hurt sumbody. These niggers will have to go back to the plantations and work. I ain't agoing to support nary one of 'em, and when you hear anybody say so, you tell 'em "it's a lie," *so-called.* I golly, I ain't got nuthin to support myself on. We fought ourselves out of every thing excepting children and land, and I suppose the land are to be turned over to the niggers for graveyards.

Well, my friend, I don't want much. I ain't ambitious, as I used to was. You all have got your shows and monkeys and sircusses and brass band and orgins, and can play on the petrolyum and the harp of a thousand strings, and so on, but I've only got one favor to ax of you. I want enough powder to kill a big yaller stump-tail dog that prowls round my premises at night. Pon honor, I won't shoot at any thing blue or black or mullater. Will you send it? Are you and your folks so skeered of me and my folks that you won't let us have any amunition? Are the squirrels and crows and black racoons to eat up our poor little corn-patches? Are the wild turkeys to gobble all around us with impunity? If a mad dog takes the hiderphoby, is the whole community to run itself to death to get out of the way? I golly! It looks like your people had all took the rebelfoby for good, and was never gwine to get over it. See here, my friend, you must send me a little powder and a ticket to your show, and me and you will harmonize sertin.

With these few remarks I think I feel better, and hope I hain't made nobody fitin mad, for I'm not on that line at this time.

I am truly your friend, all present or accounted for,

BILL ARP, *so-called.*

P. S.—Old man Harris wanted to buy my fiddle the other day with Confederit money. *He* sed it would be good agin. *He* says that Jim Funderbuk told him that Warren's Jack seen a man who had jest come from Virginny, and *he* said a man had told his cousin Mandy that Lee had whipped 'em *agin.* Old Harris says that a feller by the name of Mack C. Million is coming over with a million of men. But nevertheless, notwithstandin, somehow or somehow else, I'm dubus about the money. If you was me, Artemus, would you make the fiddle trade?

B. A.

BILL ARP ON THE STATE OF THE COUNTRY.

"Sweet land of Liberty, of thee I sing."

NOT much *I* don't, not at this time. If there's any thing sweet about liberty in this part of the vineyard, I can't see it. The land's good enough, and I wouldn't mind hearin a hyme or two about the dirt I live on, but as for findin sugar and liberty in Georgy soil, it's all a mistake. Howsumever, I'm hopeful. I'm much calmer and sereener than I was a few months ago. I begin to feel kindly towards all people, except some. I'm now endeaverin to be a great national man. I've taken up a motto of no North, no South, no East, no West; but let me tell you, my friend, I'll bet on Dixie as long as I've got a dollar. It's no harm to run both schedules. In fact it's highly harmonious to do so. I'm a good Union reb, and my battle cry is Dixie and the Union.

But you see, my friend, we are gettin restless about some things. The war had become mighty heavy on us, and after the big collapse, we thought it was over for good. We had killed folks and killed folks until the novelty of the thing had wore off, and we were mighty nigh played out all over. Children were increasin and vittels diminishin. By a close calculashun it was perceived that we didn't kill our enemies as fast as they was imported, and about those times I thought it was a pity that some miracle of grace hadn't cut off the breed of foreigners some eighteen or twenty years ago. Then you would have seen a fair fight. General Sherman wouldn't have walked over the track, and Ulyses would have killed more men than he did—*of his own side.* I have always thought that a general ought to be particular which side he was sacrifisin.

Well, if the war is over, what's the use of fillin up our towns and cities with soldiers any longer? Where's your reconstruction that the papers say is goin on so rapidly? Where's the liberty and freedom? The fact is, General Sherman and his caterpillars made such a clean sweep of every thing, I don't see much to reconstruct. They took so many liberties around here that there's nary liberty left. I could have reconstructed a thousand sich States before this. Any body could. There wasn't nothin to do but jest to go off and let us alone. We've got plenty of statesmen—plenty of men for governor. Joe Brown ain't dead—he's a waitin—standin at the door with his hat off. Then what's the soldiers here for—what good are they doin—who wants to see 'em any longer? Everybody is tired of the war, and we don't want to see any more signs of it. The niggers don't want 'em, and the white men don't want 'em, and as for the women—whoopee! I golly! Well, there's no use talking—when the stars fall agin maybe the women will be harmonized. That male bisness—that oath about gittin letters! They always was jealous about the males anyhow, and that order jest broke the camel's back. Well, I must confess that it was a powerful small concern. I would try to sorter smooth it over if I know'd what to say, but I don't. If they was afeered of the women why didn't they say so? If they wasn't what do they make 'em swear for? Jest to aggravate 'em? Didn't they know that the best way to harmonize a man, was to harmonize his wife first? What harm can the women do by receiving their letters oath free? They can't vote, nor they can't preach, nor hold office, nor play soldier, nor muster, nor wear breeches, nor ride straddle, nor cuss, nor chaw tobacco, nor do nothing hardly but talk and rite letters. I hearn that a valiant colonel made a woman put up her fan because it had a picture of Beauregard 'pon it. Well, she's harmonized, I reckon. Now the trouble of all sich is that after these bayonets leave here and go home, these petticoat tyrants can't come back any more. Some Georgia fool will mash the juice out of 'em, certain, and that wouldn't be neither harmonious nor healthy. Better let the women alone.

Then there is another thing I'm waitin for. Why

don't they reconstruct the niggers if they are ever going to? They've give 'em a powerful site of freedom, and devilish little else. Here's the big freedmen's buro, and the little buros all over the country, and the papers are full of grand orders and special orders, and paragrafs, but I'll bet a possum that some of 'em steals my wood this winter or freezes to death. Freedman's buro? freedman's humbug I say. Jest when the corn needed plowin the worst, the buro rung the bell and tolled all the niggers to town, and the farmers lost the crops, and now the freedman is gettin cold and hungry, and wants to go back, and there ain't nuthin for 'em to go to. But freedom is a big thing. Hurraw for freedom's buro! Sweet land of liberty, of thee I don't sing! But it's all right. I'm for freedom myself. Nobody wants any more slavery. If the abolitionists had let us alone we would have fixed it up right a long time ago, and we can fix it up now. The buro ain't fixed it, and it ain't a goin to. It don't know any thing about it. Our people have got a heap more feelin for the poor nigger than any abolitionist. We are as poor as Job, but I'll bet a dollar we can raise more money in Rome to build a nigger church than they did in Boston. The papers say that after goin round for three weeks, the Boston Christians raised thirty-seven dollars to build a nigger church in Savannah. They are powerful on theory, but devilish scarce in practice.

But it's no use talkin. Everybody will know by

waitin who's been foold. Mr. Johnson says he's gwine to experiment, that's all he can do now—it's all anybody can do. Mr. Johnson's head's level. I'm for him, and everybody ought to be for him—only he's powerful slow about some things. I ain't a-worshipping him. He never made me. I hear folks hollerin hurraw for Andy Johnson, and the papers say, Oh! he's for us, he's all right, he's our friend. Well, spose he is—hadn't he ought to be? Did you expect him to be a dog, or a black republican pup? Because he ain't a-hangin of us, is it necessary to be playin hipocrite around the foot-stool of power, and making out like he was the greatest man in the world, and we was the greatest sinners? Who's sorry? Who's repenting? Who ain't proud of our people? Who loves our enemies? Nobody but a durned sneak. I say let 'em hang and be hanged to 'em, before I'd beg 'em for grace. Whar's Socrates, whar's Cato? But if Andy holds his own, the country's safe, provided these general assemblys and sinods and bishop's conventions will keep the devil and Brownlow tied. Here's a passel of slink-hearted fellers who played tory just to dodge bullitts or save property, now a-howlin about for office—want every thing because they was for Union. They was for themselves, that's all they was for, and they ain't a-goin to git the offices neither. Mr. Johnson ain't got no more respect for 'em than I have. We want to trade 'em off. By hoky, we'll give two of 'em for one copperhead, and ax nothin to boot.

Let 'em shinny on their own side, and git over among the folks who don't want us reconstructed. There's them newspaper scribblers who slip down to the edge of Dixey every twenty-four hours, and peep over at us on tip-toe. Then they run back a-puffin and blowin with a straight coat tail, and holler out, "He ain't dead—he ain't dead—look out everybody! I'm jest from thar—seen his toe move—heard him grunt—he's goin to rise agin. Don't withdraw the soljers, but send down more troops immegeately." And here's your "Harper's Weekly" a-headin all sich—a-gassin lies and slanders in every issue—makin insultin pikters in every sheet—breedin everlastin discord, and chawin bigger than ever since we got licked. Wish old Stonewall had cotched these Harpers at their ferry, and we boys had knowd they was goin to keep up this devilment so long. We'd a-made baptists of them sertin, payroll or no payroll. Hurraw for a brave soldier, I say, reb or no reb, Yank or no Yank; hurraw for a manly foe and a generous victor; hurraw for our side too, I golly, excuse me, but sich expressions will work their way out sometimes, brakes or no brakes.

But I'm for Mr. Johnson. I'm for all the Johnsons—it's a bully name. There's our Governor, who ain't goin at a discount—and there's Andy, who is doing powerful well considerin, and there's the hero of Shiloh—peace to his noble ashes.

And there's Joe—my bully Joe—wouldn't I walk ten

PARADISE LOST.

p. 143.

miles of a rainy night to see them hazel eyes, and feel the grip of his soldier hand? Didn't my rooster always clap his wings and crow whenever he passed our quarters? "Instinct told him that he was the true prince," and it would make anybody brave to be nigh him. I like all the Johnsons, even to Sam—L. C. He never levied on me if he could git round it. For twenty years me and Sam have been workin together in the justice court. I was an everlastin defendant, and Sam the constable, but he never sold my property nor skeered Mrs. Arp. Hurraw for the Johnsons!

Well, on the whole, there's a heap of things to be thankful for. I'm thankful the war is over—that's the big thing. Then I'm thankful I ain't a black republican pup. I'm thankful that Thad Stevens and Sumner and Phillips, nor none of their kin, ain't no kin to *me.* I'm thankful for the high privilege of hatin all such. I'm thankful I live in Dixey, in the State of Georgia, and our Governor's name ain't Brownlow. Poor Tennessee! I golly, didn't she catch it! Andy Johnson's pardons would do rebs much good there. They better git one from the devil if they expect it to pass. Wonder what made Providence afflict 'em with sich a cuss.

But I can't dwell on sich a subject. Its highly demoralizing and unprofitable.

> "Sweet Land of Liberty, of thee
> I could not sing in Tennessee."

But then we've had a circus once more, and seen the clown play round, and that makes up for a heap of trouble. In fact, it's the best sign of rekonstruction I have yet observed.

Yours, hopin,
BILL ARP.

P. S.—And they hauled Grant's cabin a thousand miles. Well, Sherman's war-horse stayed in my stable one night. I want to sell the stall to some Yankee State Fair. As our people ain't the sort that runs after big folk's things, the stall ain't no more than any other stall to me. State Fairs, it's for sale! I suppose that "Harper's Weekly" or Frank Lesly will paint a picture of it soon by drawin on their imagination. B. A.

TO THE CHATTANOOGA GAZETTE.

GENTLE SIR: I don't think you tote fair. I haven't expressed my lacerated feelins in public but twice since the war. I didn't live in Chattanoogy, and I didn't hav no Gazette. For about three months you bullied us in your paper to your entire satisfaction. Until Mr. Johnsin sorter took up for us, you never sent a sheet to Rome that didn't hurt our feelins and bore into our hearts like a cotton gimlet. You copied from Yankee papers the meanest of their slander, and it seemed to be perfectly congenial with your sentiments.

Well, sir, we bore it like an Injun. We bore it silently and proud. We looked at our desolated land, our lonesome chimneys, our grave-yards, where you unburried our dead and sunk your rifle-pits; where you broke to fragments the iron railing, and took the very tombstones to put in your fortifications. We read your exaltations of Northern bravery and Southern treason, and we scorned you from the bottom of our hearts. Now, when of late, an humble individual makes bold to burst his biler, and express his sentiments in two brief letters, you get up like a sanctified preacher and read him a public lecture about *harmonizin.* Gentle sir, it don't become you. When I've insulted you about 2,000 times we will be even. But I don't intend to insult you at all. If you are an honest man and a generous conqueror, I ain't after you. When you make an effort to convince Mr. Harper's Weekly and the Black Republicans that our people, from General Lee and Mr. Davis down to the high privates, are just as good and brave and honorable as they are, I'll harmonize with you.

But, gentle sir, haven't you spread yourself too far from home? What have you been doin about harmonizin your own people? Our little burnt city is fast fillin up with your best citizens. Durin the war you let 'em stay, but after the war they are forced to leave. Like exiles, they are seekin refuge in Cherokee, Georgy, and there stands your paper like a *lampless, lightless* beacon on the shore, and sustains the men and measures that made 'em leave. You are seein 'em day after day desertin your State, and you look away off, and employ your pen in lecturin a poor stranger about *harmonizin.*

Gentle sir, shorten your sights. Begin to work on your home concerns, or you'll lose all your best society. They are welcome here, and we'll all stand by 'em, but then, I have always thought that every great State ought to have some good men left in it. Don't you? Gentle sir, tote fair.

Not yours,

BILL ARP.

BILL ARP ADDRESSES HIS CONSTITUENTS.

Respectable People:

I address you on this occasion with a profound admiration for the great consideration which caused you to honor me by your votes with a seat in the Senate of Georgy. For two momentus and inspirin weeks, the Legislature has been in solemn session, one of whom I am proud to be which. For several days we were engaged as scouts, making a sorter reconysance to see whether Georgy were a State or a Ingin territory, whether we were in the old Un-ion or out of it, whether me and my folks and you and your folks were somebody or nobody, and lastly, but by no means leastly, whether our poor innocent children, born durin the war, were all illegal and had to be born over agin or not. This last pint are much unsettled, but our women are advised to be calm and sereen.

My friends, our aim has honestly been to git you all back into the folds of the glorious Un-ion. Like the prodigal son we had nothin to live on, and feeling lonesome and hungry, hav been bowin and scrapin and makin apologys for five or six months. We have been standing afar off for weeks and weeks, but durn the calf do they kill for us. They know we've got nothing, for they eat up our substance, and as for putting rings on our fingers we couldn't expect it until they bring back the jewelry they carried away. I cannot say in the language of the poet, that our labor has been a labor of love, for we've had monstrous poor encouragement to be shure ; but we had all set our heads toward the Stars and Stripes, and we jintly determined that, come wool come wo, sink or swim, survive or perish, thunder or litenin, we'd slip back or sneak back, or git back somehow or somehow else, or we'd stay out forever and ever, and be hanged to 'em, so-called, I golly.

Up to this time it has been an uphill business. The team was a good one, and the gear all sound, and the wagin greased, but the road is perhaps the roughest, rottenest cordroy in the world. It's pull up and scotch, and pull up and scotch, and ever and annonymus the scotch slips out and the tongue cuts round, and away we go into the gully. Andy Jonsin is the driver, and he says, "go slow," and he hollers "wo, wo," and loses the road, and then we have to go back to the fork and wait till he blazes the way. He seems to be doing his best, but then thar is Sumner and Satin and Stevens and Davis and other like gentlemen who keep hollerin at him and crackin his whip and confusin his idees, so that sometimes we don't know whether he's gee-in or haw-in.

My friends, about them fellers I don't know what I ought to say. If you do, or if anybody does, I wish they would say it. I don't encourage cussin in nobody, not at all, but if you know of a man that can't be broke of it durin his natural life, it might be well to hire him by the year. If there is in all history a good excuse and a proper subject, it is upon them heartless, soulless, bowelless, gizzardless, fratrisidal, suisidal, parasidal, sistercidal, abominabul, contemptibul, disgustabul individuals. I sometimes think of 'em till my brain gits sorter addled, and I feel like becomin a volunteer convict of the lunatic asylorum. Charity inclines me to the opinyun that old Sumner is crazy. I think he has been gittin worse ever since he took Brooks on the brain, and it does seem like the disease has proved contagious. If they are for peace we can't fathom it in these regions. They fought us to free the poor nigger, but didn't care for the Union. The Western boys fought us for the Union, but didn't care for the nigger. By double teamin on us they licked us, and we gin it up, but now the one don't want our niggers and the other don't want our Union, and it's the hardest scedule to pleas 'em both a poor vanished people ever undertook. It's the hardest war to wind up that history records. Sumner, Satin, and Company are still a-fussin and fumin about the everlastin nigger—want him to vote and make laws and squat on a jury, and wants to prohibit us rebels from doin the same thing for thirty years to come! Jeerusalem! where is the cussin man? They say it's all right for a nigger not to vote in Connecticut, because there ain't but a few of 'em thar; and it s all wrong for 'em not to vote in Georgy, because there's a heap of 'em here, and they talk logic and rhetoric amazin to show how it is. Well, I hain't got a whole passel of sense like some, but as sure as I am two foot high a nigger is a nigger I don't care where you smell him, and a vote is a vote I don't care where you drap it. I golly, they can't git over that.

The truth is, my fellow-citizens, I sometimes feel like we didn't have no Government. I felt that way sorter when Mr. Gibson appointed me a Committee on the State of the Republic. When the Secretary read out my name all mixed up with the Republic, I felt that I was obleged to renig. Risin majestically to my feet, says I, "Mr. President, I beg to be respectfully excused, sir, if you please. If there's any Republic on this side of Jordin, I can't perceive it at this time with these specs. Thar was a place in old Virginny called Port Republic, but Mr. Rebel General Stonewall Jackson wiped out its contents generally in 1863, and I haven't since heard of it in Northern literature. I have heard of a scrub concern over about Washington they call a Republic, but, sir, it is likely to prove the grandest imposture that ever existed on a continent of freedom. I suppose, sir, it is to be moved to Boston or the infernal regions in a few days, and I want nothin to do with it. Excuse me, sir, but I must insist on being respectably discharged." I took my seat amidst the most profoundest and tumultuous silence ever seen, and Mr. Gibson remarked that he wouldn't impose the republic on no respectable man agin his wishes. He then transferred me to the finance committee, and said he hoped we would take immediate action, for the State had no money, as well as himself, and board was high and eat seteras frequent. This may not hav been his exactual language, but is anglin towards it. I bowed my head and sed "Ditto, except that I don't eat seteras." Forthwith I telegraft various gentlemen for a temporary loan, but they wouldn't lend a dollar until Mr. Jenkins war inorgarated, for they wanted his name to the note. Thinks says I there's a tap lost about this wagon. If we are a State we can borrow money in Augusta. If we ain't a State it's none of our bisiness to borrow it at all. If Andy wants to run the machine his own way, let him pay his own expences. What in the dickens is a provision government for if it ain't to get up provisions and provide for a feller generally? I made up my mind that perhaps we had been humorin Andy about long enough; we had as much right to a governor as Alabama or South Callina. He wants us back about as bad as we want to git back, and a little badder *perhaps*, and he needn't put on so many unnecessary airs about the senator bisiness. If he fools with us much, we won't elect nobody.

I golly, we'll take the studs and go backwards. I forthwith returned to the capitol, and stretching forth one of my arms says I, "Mr. Gibson, sir—I'm your friend—I'm the friend of your wife and children, but if Mr. Jenkins ain't inaugurated soon the State will collapse. A bright and glorious star will be obliterated from off the striped rag, and the President will lose about nine supporters in the Federal Congress. I move, sir, that if we can't git our governor at once like a sine qua non, we break up in a row and depart for Mexico." It took like the small pox, and was carried tumultously. These proceedins was telegrafed to Washington before the ink was dry, and we received orders forthwith to inaugurate our governor and roll on our cart. Then the money come, and we voted ourselves a pocket full a-piece and took a furlough. My friends, that was a proud and glorious day, when that great and good man was makin his affecting speech. We all felt happy, and Captain Dodd, the member from Polk, remarked that he would like to die then, for he never expected to feel as heavenly agin. The tears ran down his left eye like rain. His other eye was beat out by a Yankee soldier while the cappen was in prison. Of course the villain was tried for it and hung, though I hain't seen no mention of it in the papers. Alas poor Wirz!

My fellow-people, let me in conclusion congratulate you on having a governor once more, as is a governor. Oh there is life in the old land yet, and by and by we'll transport them black Republicans into the African desert, and put 'em to teaching Hottentots the right of suffrage. Winter Davis could then find a field of labor sufficient for the miserable remnant of his declining years. He is the Winter of our discontent, and we want to git rid of him. He and his clan have done us much evil, and I am induced to exclaim in the language of Paul about Alexander, the coppersmith, "May the Lord reward 'em accordin to their works." More anonymous,

BILL ARP.

P. S.—Cousin John Thrasher says he studied law for a week, and will be a candidate for some high office when we meet again, provided we give him time to sell his cotton seed. I'll say this for him, art has done as much for him as for some of the candidates, and nature more, and his cotton seed are as good seed as I ever seed. I hope he will suck-seed. B. A.

BILL ARP TO HIS OLD FRIEND.

MR. JOHN HAPPY—

SIR: I want to write to you personally about some things that's weighin on me. I look on you as a friend, and I feel like dropping a few lines by way of unburthening my sorrowful reflections. For the last few years you have travelled round right smart, and must have made a heap of luminous observations. I hear you are now living in Nashville, where you can see all sides of every thing, and read all the papers, where you can study Paradise Lost without a Book, and see the devil and his angels, without drawing on the imagination, and I thought maybe you might assist me in my troubled feelings. I have always, Mr. Happy, endeavored to see the bright side of every picture if it had any, but there is one or two subjects about which I had mighty nigh giv it up.

I want you to tell me if you can, about what time are the black republicans goin to quit persecuting our people? What are they so everlastin mad with us about? Old Skewball says it's for treason that we've gone and done, and that I'm the slowest perceving man he ever saw not to have found it out.

Now treason is a mighty bad thing, and any man found guilty of treason ought to be talked to by a preacher right under a gallows, and then be allowed to stand on nothing for a few hours by the clock. Shore enough treason I mean. Treason where a man slips around on the sly in time of war, and takes sides agin his country. Jest as though, for instance, I should have worked agin my sovereign State after she had seceded, and had stole her powder or deserted her in her time of peril, while she was defendin herself against the combined assaults of the world, the flesh and the devil. I wouldn't have blamed nobody for hangin me for the like, would you? But Skewball says we ain't got no sovereign States—that the war has settled the question agin us on that point. I don't think so, my frend. I admit that we ain't nothin in particular now, but we did have sovereign States before the war, and the sword ain't settled nor unsettled no great principles. There ain't no trial of right or wrong by wager of battle nowadays. For mity nigh a hundred years this country has been a big debatin society on these questions. From the time of Hamilton and Jefferson down to 1861, the right of a State to dissolve her own partnership has been argued by powerful minded men, and there has been more for it than agin it. More Presidents, more senators, more statesmen, more judges, more people. Massachusetts and Connecticut were for it at one time, and bellered round and pawed dirt amazin to git out, but they found out Barcus was willin and they didn't go. I believe, however, that old Nutmeg did stay out about two hours and a half.

Well, the South went out mighty unwillingly, Mr. Happy, as you know. She had been mighty nigh kicked out for a long time, and there was a big party that wanted us to go out and stay out. Everybody knows we didn't get along in peace, so we concluded to do like Abraham and his brother-in-law; to separate our households. What they wanted to keep us for I never could see, and can't see yet. I wouldn't have a nigger or a dog to stay round me that didn't want to. Some say they wanted us to strengthen them agin their enemies in case of a furrin war. Does any man in his senses expect us to help the Black Republicans whip any body? Have we got any worse enemies than they are? They can't make us fight, I reckon, if we don't want to. We've fought enough, and made nothing by it but glory, and we ain't agoing to join in another war to gratify other people. Dodds says before he'd pull a trigger for Thad Stevens, he'd have his soul transmigrated to a bench-leg'd fice, and bark at his daddy's mules 2,000 years. I wonder if the experience of the last four years ain't satisfied these fellows that our boys are a dangerous set to be turned loose in time of war. Wouldn't you think that as a matter of policy they would soft sodder us a little, and quit their slanderin? If we do fight for 'em, there will be one condition certain—they mout be put where David put Uriah, and our boys mout consent to make a charge or two behind 'em at the point of the bagnet.

But I want you to tell me, John, if I am right about the history of this business. It ain't a long story, and I'll tell it the way I see it. Old Pewrytan went off one day with some ships, and took a few beads and Jews harps, and bought up a lot of captured niggars from the Hottentots, or some other tots, and stole a few more on the coast of Africa, and brought 'em over and educated 'em to work in the field, and cut wood, and skeer bars, and so forth, but not includin votin, nor musterin, nor the jury business, nor so forth.

Well, after while they found that the cold winds and codfish airs of New England didn't agree with the nigger, and so they begun to slide 'em down South as fast as possible. After they had sold 'em, and got the money, they jined the Church, and became sanctified about slavery, sorter like the woman that got converted and then give all her novels away to her unconverted sister. Well, the Old Dominion, and sich of her sons as Washington, and Jefferson, and Madison, and Randolph, bought 'em and worked 'em to satsifaction; whereupon Old Pew got jealous and began to preach agin it to break it down. After while they went into the striped almanak bisness, makin bloody picturs of poor lascerated niggers gettin a hundred lashes for nothin, and mournin for their first-born because they were not. Then they started the stealin prograghm, and while we were tryin all the big courts and little courts to git back one sickly melatter, by the name of Dred Scott, they were stealin from five to fifty a day, and coverin their carcasses all over with nigger larceny, and smuglin the Constitution into an abolishun mush. They built a fence around the institution as high as Haman's gallows, and hemmed it in, and laid siege to it jest like an army would besege a city to starve out the inhabitants. They kept peggin at us untell we got mad—shore enuff mad—and we resolved to cut loose from 'em, and paddle our own canoo.

Now, all this time, we had some good frends among 'em—some who swore we were imposed upon, and said we had good cause to dissolve the partnership. They said that if we did seseed, and the abolishunests made war upon us, they would stand by us and throw their lives and fortunes and their sacred honor right into the breach, and the first fight would be over their dead bodies, and so on. My memory is bad, but I remember that some of 'em were named James Buchanan, and Dan Dickinson, and John Cochran, and Logan, and Cushin, and Butler, surnamed the Beast, and McLernard, and Stephen A. Douglas, who got his commission about the time he died, and carried it with him to parts unknown; and lastly, a man by the name of Andy Johnson, who, I suppose, are some distant relation to the President of the United States of America.

But a man ain't responsible for the bad conduct of his relations, and I don't throw it up to nobody. I suppose that our President are doin the best he can, and Mr. Ethridge oughtn't to be taking up his record.

Well, the war come on, and shore enuff, Logan and Cushin and McLernard and Butler and Company buzzed around a while like bumble-bees, till they were bought up, and then they lit over on the other side. They got their reward, and they are welcome to it so far as I am concerned.

How is it now, Mr. Happy? They conquered us by the sword, but they haven't convinced us of nuthin much that I know of. All is lost save honor, and that they can't steal from us nor tarnish.

If they had held out the hand of fellowship, we would have made friends and buried the hatchet. But the very minit they whipped us, they begun to holler *treason* from one end of the country to the other just like they had made a bran new discovery. It seemed to strike 'em all of a sudden like Xpost facto law, and they wanted to go into a general hangin bisness, and keep it up as long as they could find rope and timber.

Now, the idea of several millions of American freemen being guilty of treason at once! The idea of applyin treason to the Old Dominion, the mother of States, and of Washington and Jefferson and Madison and Marshall and Patrick Henry and all the Lees, and who give away all the territory in the Northwest for nuthin! Is she to be scandalized by these new-light Christians who are compounded from all the skum of all creation, and think that Paul and Peter and Revelations have been for two hundred years makin special arrangements for receivin their sanctified souls in Paradise? Treason the dickens! Where's your dictionary? Where's Dan'l Webster? Where's the history of the American Revolution?

No, it ain't treason or reason—but it's devellish, infernal, inhuman hate. What do they keep Mr. Davis in jail for? I hear sum say that it ain't Mr. Johnson's voluntary doings, but the tremengius pressure of surrounding circumstances. Durn the circumstances. Ain't Mr. Davis a great and good man? If Andy Johnson ain't an infidel, wouldn't he swap chances for heaven with him, and give all his earthly estate to boot? If Mr. Davis's honor and integrity and patriotism and true courage were weighed in a balance against Sumner's and Stevens's and all his enemies, wouldn't he outweigh 'em all? Won't his conduct in Mexico, and in the late war, and his nobility of character, live long, and grow bright in history, while the memory of the hounds that are bayin him in his dungeon will sink into oblivion? I think so—that's what I say, and I'll bet on it, and Charles O'Conor and all the women in the country will go my halves.

But there ain't no particular point in all this, Mr. Happy. It's only my opinion, that's all. I may be a tarnal fool, and I sometimes feel like I am a fool about every thing, and don't know nothin. I'm tryin my best, however, to take things jest as I find 'em, and my principal business for the last two months have been weanin' niggers to make 'em feel free. I put 'em all out to take care of themselves, and I don't know what Thad Stevens is a-fussin about, unless he is jest mad because our boys burnt his iron-works. If that's all, we can plead the ruins of various similar establishments in these regions, and get a judgment against him.

But I'm about through, Mr. Happy, with what I had to say. Only this—if there ever was an afflicted people that needed friends, it's us. If we've got any friends anywhere, I want 'em to show their hands and stand by us in our trouble. I feel like reachin out to the five points of the compass in search of sympathy, and if there is an honest statesman or a brave soldier north of the line who loves his fellow-men, let him open his heart and meet us on half-way ground. We ain't afeered of beasts or varmints—of devils or demons—of Stevens or Sumner—but we are a warm-hearted and forgivin people, and friends. Ain't we, and don't we?

Yours, everlastingly,

BILL ARP.

P. S.—Is Brownlow dead yet? I'm writin his obituary, and thought I would like for the sad event to come off as soon as possible. I wish you would send me a list of your members who voted for that resolution declarin General Lee and Mr. Davis infamous. We are gettin up a bill in the Georgy Legislater, declarin *them* infamous who voted for the resolution. Fight the devil with fire is my motto.

B. A.

BILL ARP ADDRESSES THE LEBANON LAW SCHOOL AND GIVES HIS OWN SAD EXPERIENCE.

MILLEDGEVILLE, *February*, 1866.

MESSRS. C. C. CUMMINGS AND OTHERS, COMMITTEE—

GENTLEMEN: I have received your kind invitation to address your law school. In the situation by which I am surrounded it is impossible for me to go. I wish I could, for I would like to tell you all I know about law, and it wouldn't take me long. I'm now in the law bisness myself, at this place. We are engaged in manufacturin it by wholesale, and after while it will be retailed out by the lawyers to anybody that wants it. It's an easy bisness to make law, though some of the bills introduced are awfully spelt. To-day I saw a bill in which "masheenry" was spelt with two esses and four ease. But the greatest difficulty is in understandin the law after it is made. Among lawyers this difficulty don't seem to lie so much in the head as in the pocket. For five dollars a lawyer can luminize some, and more akkordin to pay. But he oughtn't to luminize but one side at a time. The first case I ever had in a justice court I employed old Bob Leggins, who was a sorter of a self-educated fool. I give him two dollars in advance, and he argued the case, as I thought, on two sides, and was more luminous agin me than for me. I lost the case, and found out afterwards that the defendant had employd Leggins after I did, and give him five dollars to lose my case. I look upon this as a warnin to all clients to pay big fees and keep your lawyer out of temptation.

My experience in litigation have not been satisfactory. I sued Sugar Black onst for the price of a load of shucs. He said he wanted to buy some ruffness, and I agreed to bring him a load of shucs for two dollars. My wagin got broke, and he got tired a-waitin, and sent out after the shucs himself. When I calld on him for the pay, he seemd surprisd, and said it had cost him two dollars and a half to have the shucs hauled, and that I justly owed him a half a dollar. He was bigger than I was, so I swallowed my bile and sued him. His lawyer plead a set-off for haulin. He plead that the shucs was unsound; that they were barrd by limitations; that they didn't agree with his cow, and that he never got any shucs from me. He spoke about an hour, and allouded to me as a swindler about forty-five times. The bedevild jury went out and brought in a verdict again me for fifty cents and four dollars for costs of suit. I hain't saved nary shuc on my plantation since, and I don't intend to until it gits less expensive. I look upon this as a warnin to all folks *never to go to law about shucs*, or any other small circumstance.

The next trouble I had wus with a feller who I hired to dig me a well. He wus to dig it for twenty dollar, and I wus to pay him in meat and meal, and sich like. The vagabond kept gittin along until he got all the pay, but hadn't dug nary foot in the groun. So I made out my akkount, and sued him as follers, to wit:

Old John Hanks to Bill Arp.	*Dr.*
To 1 Well you didn't dig	$20.

Well, Hanks he hired a cheap lawyer, who rard round extensively, and sed a heap of funny things at my expense, and finally dismissed my case for what he called its "ridikulum absurdum." I paid those costs, and went home a sadder and a wiser man. I pulled down my little cabin, and moved it some 300 yards nigher to the spring, and I've drunk mity little well-water since. I look upon this case as a warnin to all folks *never to pay for any thing till you've got it, espeshially if it has to be dug.*

The next law case I had I gained it all by myself by the force of circumstances. I bought a man's note that was given for the hire of a nigger boy, Dik. Findin he wouldn't pay me, I sued him before old Squire McGinnis, beleevin it was sich a dead thing that the devil couldn't keep me out of a verdik. The feller's attorney plead failure of consideration, and *non est faktum* and *ignis fatuis*,

YANKEE DOODLE.

p. 129.

and infancy, and that the nigger's name wasn't *Dik*, but *Richard*. The old squire was a powerful secesh, and hated the Yankees amazin. So, after the lawyer had got through his speech and finished up his readin from a book called "Greenleaf," I rose forward to an attitood. Stretchin forth my arm, ses I, "Squire McGinnis, I would ask, sir, if this is a time in the history of our afflicted country when Federal law books should be admitted in a Southern patriot's court? Haven't we seceeded for ever from their foul domination? Don't our flag wave over Fort Sumter, and what, sir, have we got do with Northern laws? On the very first page of the gentleman's book I seed the name of the city of Boston. Yes, sir, it was written in Boston, published in Boston, and sold in Boston, where they don't know no more about the hire of a nigger than an ox knows the man who will tan his hide." I sed some more things that was pinted and patriotic, and closed my argument by handin the book to the squire. He put on his spektakles, and after lookin at the book about a minute, says he:

"Mr. Arp, you can have a judgment, and I hope that from henceforth and for ever no lawyer will presume to come before this honorable court with pisen documents to prove his case. If he do, this court will take it as a insult, and send him to jail."

I look upon this case as a warnin to all folks who gamble in law, to hold a good hand and play it well. High jestice and patriotism are winnin trumps.

8

After this I had a difficulty with a man by the name of Kohen, and I thought I wouldn't go to law, but would arbytrate. I had bought Tom Swillins' wheat at a dollar a bushel, *if he couldn't do any better*, and if he could do better, he was to cum back and *give me the preference.* The skamp went off and sold the wheat to Kohen for a dollar and five cents, and Kohen knowd all about his contrakt with me. Me and him like to have fit, and perhaps would, if I hadn't been puny ; but we finally left it all to Josh Billins to arbytrate. Old Josh deliberated on the thing for three days and nights, and finally brot in an award that Kohen should have the wheat and *I should have the preference.* I hain't submitted no more cases to arbitration since, and my advice to all peepul is to arbytrate nuthin if your case is honest, for there ain't no judge there to keep one man from trikin the other. An honest man don't stand no chance nowhere exseppin in a court house with a good lawyer to back him. The motto of this case is, never to arbytrate nuthin but a bad case, and take a good lawyer's advice, and pay him for it before you do that.

But I got Fretman—*I* didn't, but my lawyer Marks did. Fretman was a nutmeg skoolteacher who had gone round my naborhood with his skool artikles, and I put down for Troup and Calhoun to go, and intended to send seven or eight more if he proved himself right. I soon found that the little nullifier's learnin wasn't in any thing, and on inquiry I found that Nutmeg was givin powerful long receesses, and was employin his time chiefly in carryin on with a tolerabul sizd female gal that was goin to him. Troup sed he heard the gal squeel herself one day, and he knowd Fretman was a-squeezin of her. I don't mind our boy's squeezin of the Yankee gals, but I'll be blamed if the Yankees shall be a-squeezin ourn. So I got mad and took the childern away. At the end of the term Fretman sued me for eighteen dollars, and hired a cheap lawyer to collekt it. Before this time I had learned some sense about a lawyer, so I hired a good one, and spred my pocket-book down before him, and told him to take what would satisfy him. And he tuk. Old Phil Davis was the jestice. Marks made the openin speech to the effek that every professional man ought to be able to illustrate his trade, and he therefore proposed to put Mr. Fretman on the stand and *spell him.* This motion were fout hard, but it agreed with old Phil's notions of "high jestice," and says he, "Mr. Fretman, you will have to spell, sir." Marks then swore him that he would give true evidence in this case, and that he would spell every word in Dan'l Webster's spellin book correkly to the best of his knowledge and belief, so help him, etc. I saw then that he wer tremblin all over like a cold wet dog. Says Marks, "Mr. Fretman, spell 'tisik;'" well, he spelt it, putting in a *ph* and a *th* and a *gh* and a *zh*, and I don't know what all, and I thought he was gone up the first pop, but Marks said it was right. He then spelt him right strait along on all sorts of big words, and little words, and long words, and short words, and afterwords, and he knowd 'em all, till finally Marks ses, "Now, sir, spell *Ompompynusuk*." Fretman drawd a long breth, and sed it wasn't in the book. Marks proved it was by an old preacher, who was settin by, and old Phil spoke up with power, ses he, "Mr. Fretman, you must spell it, sir." Fretman was a swettin like a run-down filly. He tuk one pass at it, and *missd*.

"You can come down, sir," says Marks, "you've lost your case." And shore enuf, old Phil give a verdict aginst him like a darn.

Marks was a whale in his way. At the same court he was about to nonsuit a doctor bekause he didn't have his diplomy, and the doctor begd the court for time to go home after it. He rode seven miles and back as hard as he could lick it, and when he handed it over to Marks very triumfantly, Marks ses, "Now, sir, you will take the stand and translate this Latin into English, so that the court may understand it." Well, he jest caved, for he couldn't do it.

He lost his case in two minets, for the old squire said that a doctor who couldn't read his diplomy had no more right to practise than a magistrate who couldn't read the license had to jine two couple together. This is a warnin to all perfessional men to understand their bisness, and the moral of the case is, that a man oughtn't to be squeezin the gals when anybody can see him. But I don't want it understood that I'm agin it on proper occasions and in a tender manner. There ain't no squeelin necessary.

But I must close this brief epistle.

Yours, truly,

BILL ARP.

BILL ARP TO MR. TAMMANY HALL.

MILLEDGEVILLE, *February*, 1866.

DEAR TAMMANY: You are a glorious old feller. You've got a heart—a great big heart—and if you were here, I would exclaim, in the langdwage of my unkle Billy, "put your hand in mine, honey, and kiss me." We are whipd at last, old Tammany. We rebs are conquered, subdued, and subjugated, not by bayonets or bullets, but by your friendly overtures, your manly speeches. You and Sunny South Cox and Company have captured us, taken us prisoners, and we are now as dosile as we have been hostile. Didn't I tell you that we would meet you on half-way grown? Didn't we stretch forth our arms for sympathy, and wasn't we about to turn away in defiance and despair for the want of it?

"*We spread the mantle of oblivion over the past. If you of the South have the spirit to accept, we of the North have the heart to tender you the offices of kindness. We will help you plant again the seed whose perfect leaves, flowers, and fruits shall be yours with ours to enjoy.*"

Did Mr. Cox say that, old Tammany, and did you clap your hands and say encore?

"*We are to-day arrayed against the contention concerning the black race, and are looking forward to the white race for the welfare and greatness of our country.*"

And didn't you say that, too, old Tammany? and didn't all hands jewbilee and exclaim, "that's it, them's 'em, that's the doktrine, the nigger may be a big fish, but the white man is a whale." And didn't you all take another drink on that, Mr. Tammany? Wish some of us rebs had been there, old fel, jest to have techd tumblers with you. Thank the Lord that there are good men north of Dixey. There's a heap of 'em here, Mr. Hall, and their hearts are jumpin and a-bumpin and a-thumpin as big as yours. Their hearts were castles, and their bosoms citadels, but you have taken 'em. Don't be alarmed, don't receed, don't take back nothin; be calm and sereen, and we of the rebellious South will wipe out the last spark of hatred to such as you. We are now wipin away the curses that were upon our lips. We are rising up from our humiliation, and like strong men are shakin the dust from our garments. Think of it, Tammany. What a glorious sight to see a brave peepul lifted up—a whole nation of white folks reconsiled! What spirit, what ghost, what inspiration told you how to reach us? How did you know that we was weak where we was strong in the same secret corner of our bosoms?

You've got us, Tammany, and we'll respond to you; we'll reinforce you. We've said some hard things, Mr. Hall; we've tried to scorch and blister and excoriate, but you see we were goaded, gored by bulls—Trumbulls and Republican bulls. They bellerd and we pawed dirt. They punched us in the cage, and we growled. They put tacks under our saddles, and we kicked. What else could we do? Jest think of it, Tammany. Ruined and desolate, the people in mournin, and their homes in ashes—no luxuries, no comforts, no Christmas worth a cus, no Santa Claus, no nuthin. Could we lick the hand that laid us low?—nary time—no, never. While we was strugglin to rise from out the wreck, to breathe the air above us, to take an invoice, and see if there was enough left to live for, our enemies were a-shoutin, "Hit him, kick him, mash him, smash him agin."

We were then at the bottom, Tammany. We didn't know there was any lower deep, but our enemies were huntin, and they still are huntin some deeper pit to put us in, and some pendulum of Poe to swing and cut us. Well, we ain't heathens, we've been to meetin, we've seen missionaries, we've got churches and sermons and hymn-books and prayers. We've got pious old men and women, and brave boys, and maidens who are finished all the way up like the corners of a temple. God bless 'em, Tammany, particular them last, for in connection with them are centerd the hope of posterity, and the joys of our life. We've all got hearts, old Tammany, and there's many a good Samaritan among us who wouldn't pass you by and go over on the other side. We've got charity, too, and long suffering, and patience, and hope in abundance, though we can't believe them Radicals will walk right straight into heaven without knockin at the door. That doctrine of election is a powerful thing, Tammany, but, as sure as you are born, it looks sorter unconstitutional *to us* for them fellers to enter the celestial city. They may pass amendments enough to do it, and I reckon that's why they are a-tinkerin at the old document so long; but somehow or other, when I hear one of 'em a-dyin, my thoughts naturally have a downward tendency. I can't help it, Tammany.

But, maybe we'll get over sich feelins. My wife says we will *after while.* We are all right towards you, old Hall, and our Legislature have been tryin for about two months to harmonize things generally, and any reasonable man ought to be satisfied with the efforts they have made. But, we can't satisfy them Radicals, I don't care what we do. We elected Mr. Stevens and Herchel Johnsin to the Senate, and they are mad about that. They wanted Josh Hill and Jeems Johnsin bacaus they was *Union.* Well, now, Mr. Tammany, it's better always to take men who have done somethin than men who have done nothin. Mr. Hill delivered his farewell address before he was beat, and he said he would like to know why we sing hosanna to Andy

Johnsin, who fought agin us, and yet we won't elect him who didn't. That's what's the matter, Joshua; if I may be allowed to apostrophize you, you didn't take no side at all. You say you can take the test oath and git in. Well, I don't see how, exactly. You run for Governor in sixty-three, and you writ a letter agin reconstruction, and compared the old Union *to a porcelain vase that was broke,* and couldn't never be mended agin—no, never.

And don't you know if you'd been elected you would have had to take the oath of office, and be swore to support the Constitution of the Confederate States so called, now deceased. But you are smart, Joshua, and it was funny what you said to the General that night, when he ax'd you if you would have taken that oath. You paus'd, Joshua, for nearly a minute. It was a mighty tight question, considerin the porcelain vase that was broke. I don't blame you for pausin, my friend. Finally, says you, "Well —General—I—I—didn't—much—expect—to—be—elected." Bully for you, Joshua. But now about that see-saw bisness you spoke of; you said in your speech that you was playin see-saw in politics, and if your end of the plank went down in Georgy, it would go up in Washington, by which I suppose you meant that you was ready to swap ends jest to suit your peculiar sercumstance; and that's what's the matter agin, Joshua. You have been see-sawin too long, and changin ends too often. 'Twasn't no time to be swappin hosses, my friend.

But, see here, Joshua, Mr. Marshall may be a clever reporter, but he treated you badly. , He's left out a heap of your speech. He ain't had printed that see-saw figure at all, and it was, I assure you, a most beautiful metaphor of speech. And he's left out them little sparks of Southern patriotism which you emitted. Howsomever, may be these things would have been in the way of the *Washington* end of the see-saw. I'll tell you, my friend, where you wasted time in your remarks. You said that, if we didn't elect you now, we might want you hereafter, and then we couldn't git you. Don't worry yourself on our account. Don't cross the bridge before you get to it. It will be time enough, Joshua, for you to refuse when we ask you. We haven't been runnin you down to give you office, and we ain't a-goin to. Do you see-saw away on your plank, and take good care that you don't fall off. Your speech was sorter spiteful, Joshua, and if reduced to its gum would read about thus: "Boys, *I'm* a whale, *I* am, and I'm a prophet, and if you don't elect me to the Senate, I'll go to Washington, and give you the devil."

Well, we didn't elect him, Mr. Tammany, and the devil may come. In the language of Patrick Henry, "let him come,"—I repeat it, sir, "let him come." There was another candidate, Mr. Hall, whose name was Jeems Johnsin. Well, I like Jeems purty well. He didn't run nobody down, nor put on airs. I might have voted for him, if he had lived in the State, and I hadn't liked Herchel better.

The truth is, I was partial to Jeems for his "old lang syne." He was a powerful war-horse in 'sixty-one. How glorious he figured at the Columbus war meeting. He encouraged the boys amazin, and he beat anybody a-getting volunteers. How proud we was of him that night, when he and Colonel Sims made friends on the stand, and the Colonel pind a seceshion cockade upon Jeems' coat-collar. He then got inspired, and spoke for two hours in words that breathed of ditches and death, and was full of the spirit of '76. His watch-words were "Benning and seceshion," and he voted for 'em both. Oh! he's a whale in gettin up a war. Alas! he were *sic semper* then, but he are *sic transit* now. So mote it be, Mr. Tammany; I couldn't help it. Howsomever, it don't matter much, I reckon, for we've got another Johnsin, and they are a high-roostin family, shore.

Now you understand the trouble, Mr. Tammany, about this election. We was huntin for two *full-blooded* Union men, who could find their way to Washington and back without a way-bill, and we couldn't find 'em. They ain't in the State, I tell you. So we fell back upon the old land marks, we are ridin the old wagin hosses, and our opinion is, that Andy won't raise any row in particular about it. *If he does, we don't care a darn.*

Yours truly,

BILL ARP.

P. S.—I'm gittin to be highly loyal, Mr. Hall; I know

CASABIANCA. p. 100.

I am; for a feller tried to sell me a little nigger to-day, *and I wouldn't buy him.* I heard of a bill that's comin up to bind out the niggers for 99 years, and I'm agin it. Darnd if I'll vote for more than 50. You can tell Thad. Stevens of these hopeful signs.

B. A.

ROMANCE OF THE WAR—A TRUE STORY.

COLONEL B. was my beau-ideal of a noble and gallant officer. Thanks to the good Lord for his life, for it was an unexpected boon. We never thought he would go through safe, and we listened to hear of his death or looked to see him fall in every battle. Wounded when a Lieutenant, when a Captain, when a Major, he finally had a Minié ball put through his head the day after he received his promotion as Colonel. My heart sunk down —all hearts sunk down—for we felt that the long-expected blow had come. We carried him to the rear and laid him upon the grass. The ball entered on the side of his face between the eye and ear, coming out on the opposite side in the same relative position. We thought he would soon leave us and be mingling with the spirits of other heroes in the unknown land, but the surgeon assured us the wound was not necessarily mortal, and we sent runners in search of an ambulance and a habitation.

They soon returned successful in the search, and we removed him a few miles distant, to the house of a widow who seemed anxious to do something for suffering humanity. Leaving the surgeon with him until morning, we returned to the regiment, and were soon hurried off in forced marches to complete the dear-bought victory.

Months rolled on, and we heard nothing of our Colonel. The war closed, and on my return to Charlottesville I heard that he had recovered and gone to his home in Georgia, but had enterely lost his sight. Blind! blind!—alas, I cannot say that I would have felt sadder to have heard of his death. So young, so handsome, so hopeful, must he grope in darkness for long and weary years, be led by the hand from place to place, and never again see the glad faces, the sunlit eyes of those he loves?

In the fall of last year I had occasion to visit New Orleans upon business. On my return I came through Georgia, and knowing my friend had formerly lived near the city of M., I made inquiry concerning him, and learned that he was living with his mother, a few miles from the city. On arriving at the hotel I ordered a conveyance, and when the driver learned my destination he told me that the Colonel was in the city with his own carriage, and it would be driven to the hotel in a few miuutes. Our meeting was a glorious one, especially to me, for I had so long thought of him as blind, that I felt, as I looked into his living, beaming eyes, as though he had just risen from the dead. He was surprised that I had not heard from him.

"Yes," said he, "I have been blind, totally blind. For nearly three long months I never saw even the light of day. The inflammation which proceeded from my wound affected the optic nerves, and gave me immeasurable pain and suffering. I remained, where you left me, for several weeks, and was tenderly and kindly nursed. When able to travel I telegraphed to a friend in Augusta, who came on at once and attended me home. But it is all over now, and I thank our good Father for both life and light. I had bargained with Fate to lose the latter in battle—to be mangled or crippled—but I had not bargained for perpetual blindness. I had never thought of it, and the reality when it came, I assure you, was terrible. I was greatly depressed and humiliated, but the misfortune has proved an inestimable blessing, for out of the darkness there came a light which I had never before seen—the light of dependence upon our Creator—the light of Christian love. I believe if the world was blind, they would soon learn to see into their own hearts. Did you ever know a blind man, George, who was an infidel or an atheist, or one who was even profane or wicked?

"I cannot recall one just now," said I; "but is it not equally true of all misfortunes? Do they not universally lead us to self-contemplation and self-distrust?"

"In a great measure," replied the Colonel, "but never so

much or so effectual as blindness! Oh, what a blessed thing is sight! How little prized by those who never knew its loss! Even to be deprived of it for a season is more effectual for good than all the teachings and prayers of friends or ministers. It is a perpetual reminder of our utter dependence upon a Superior Power. As it is the most valued of all our faculties, so its loss is the most impressive. Lost property can be regained, lost limbs supplied, lost health restored. And yet with the loss of all these, the eye, unclouded and bright, dallies and toys with the beautiful world. It rests only in sleep, to open again with the dawn, and feast upon the luxuries of art and nature, charm itself with the faces of relatives and friends, to catch from the eye of others the inspiration of love and gladness, or by reading, to drink into the soul the thoughts and feelings of others. No, George, the loss of sight has no compensation in this life. As you say, however, all afflictions are but blessings in disguise, and their natural tendency is to draw us heavenward. Humiliating and sad is this frailty of the heart—this forgetfulness of the Creator when He is showering upon us every thing that we need, and the remembrance of Him when he takes it away. Such is, however, the result of experience and observation, and it was a foolish error in the wife of Job to have expected her husband to curse God and die, because of his afflictions."

When we arrived at his mother's residence, I was

struck with the beauty and taste of all its surroundings. The dwelling was a Southern cottage, set like a jewel in evergreens and shade, and every thing betokened simplicity and elegance. We sat down in the spacious veranda, the Colonel remarking that the ladies had gone visiting, and we could enjoy ourselves until their return in rehearsing over Virginia scenes and campaigns.

"Well, tell me, Colonel," said I, "how you got along after we left you at Mrs. May's. Did you find good nurses and attention there?"

"The best in the world, George—I will tell you all about it, for it is a story I dearly love to recall. For a few days after you left me I was almost entirely unconscious of every thing. As my perceptions returned, my eyesight grew dim, and in a short time I was totally blind. An old man who had been a physician in his youth, lived near by, and after the surgeon left me, he came over twice a day to see me and minister to my wants. My chief attendants were Mrs. May and her daughter Fanny. I never saw either of them to remember them while I remained there, but I knew them well by their voices, their walk, yes, even their touch. Frequently they would noiselessly change the towel on my temples, when I seemed asleep, and strange as it may seem, although both were as gentle and kind as it were possible to be, yet I could tell instantly which one was bathing my burning eyes or dressing the suppurating wound. I am not altogether a convert to spiritualism George, but I tell you there is an inner sight, an instinct, an intuition which is a spiritual sense. What do you think of it?"

"I think there is," said I, "and his name is Cupid. You were in love with Miss Fanny, and I have no doubt imagined her hovering over you like an angel many a time when it was her mother."

"You are an incurable unbeliever, George," replied the Colonel; "but I will not argue with you. As I slowly recovered from the partial concussion of my brain, I began to converse with my unknown friends, and tried to learn something of their history. In this I did not succeed. The very failure increased my interest in them, and, as I acquired strength and the power of thought, I found myself unconsciously rejoicing when it chanced to be Miss Fanny who was waiting upon me. They were ladies of refinement and education, and the old Doctor congratulated me more than once on falling into their hands. 'They were raised in luxury, sir,' said he, 'but the old man died out of it. He failed, sir. He was too generous—his heart was too big, and the loss of his fortune killed him. But his widow is a lady, sir, a noble lady; and Miss Fanny is worth a million, a whole million, money or no money. If you could see her you'd think so.' This speech of the Doctor did not lessen my interest, and I almost regretted that I had telegraphed my friend to come after me.

"The day before he came, I ventured to ask Miss Fanny

if she did not have a brother, for I remembered a remark of the Doctor in which he alluded to him. She answered with much emotion, 'I had, sir, but he is dead, he was killed at Manassas.' I felt the quivering of her heart in the very pressure of her hand upon the bandage. Instinctively I placed my hand upon hers, while the most tender sympathy filled my whole soul. She did not remove it until, overcome with sad memories, she left the room.

"George, my friend, I assure you that I felt inexpressibly sad when I had to leave them. I bade the mother an affectionate adieu, and ventured to raise Miss Fanny's hand to my lips. I thought her almost inaudible 'God bless you' had the tone and tenderness of something more than ordinary regret at my departure; I did not know that I loved the girl until I had gone, and it seemed to me that my love grew stronger with every mile that separated us. But I will pass over that. When I reached home, my physician kept me confined to a dark room for a fortnight. One morning he ventured to remove the bandage from my eyes, and to my joy and surprise I saw him before me as in a mist. A month more, and my sight was pronounced perfectly restored, and the first use I made of it was to write Miss Fanny a letter—a love-letter, such a one as I had never before written, nor ever expected to write. She has returned it to me, and just for amusement I will get it and read it to you. If you ever find yourself in a similar situation, I will let you have a copy."

What does all this mean, thought I, as the Colonel went in for the letter? If she returned the letter, she must have declined him. Loved another, I suspect; but then, he is even now perfectly enraptured over her.

In a moment he returned, and seating himself beside me, he read the following:

"I am no longer blind, dear lady, and I imagine that you and your kind mother are both surprised and pleased at the announcement. Sincerely grateful to both Heaven and you, I feel it a sacred duty to devote the first moments of my recovered sight to penning with my own hand something that will express my esteem to those who were to me a mother and sister during the greatest trial and suffering of my life The merest accident made me an inmate of your house, a recipient of your tender charity. While partially unconscious of every thing around me, I imagine that I was childish and troublesome, and gave you much inconvenience and perplexing care. When my reason was restored, I was still hopeless, for I was blind. In those dark days your words of kindness lifted from me a weight of both mental and physical suffering, your voice touched me like music touches the grieved spirit. I imagined that I could see the sweet face, the sunny smile, and even now I have in my fancy two pictures that, were I an artist, I could paint to the life, and feast my eyes and heart upon the canvas.

"But I will not oppress you with gratitude—refinement

and virtue know full well when it is felt, and tenderly appreciate it, but its lavish expression is most singularly painful. I will refrain from it, Miss Fanny, but you must allow me to say something about another sentiment that has been my constant hope and comfort since I left you. I hardly knew then that my esteem and gratitude had blended into love. Do not be shocked, dear lady, but accept as true the soft confession. It is the truth—the earnest truth. I write it with deliberation, with composure, with courage—I love to write it, to think it, to dream it. In truth, I have been of late living a dreamer's life. With eye in utter darkness, it was sometimes difficult to tell whether I were asleep or awake, and in those waking moments I ever found myself 'dreaming of thee,' my spirit was polarized, and the magnet was where I left you. Continually, continually have I been drawn by some delicious influence to the hour, the moment, when I placed your hand to my lips and heard you say, 'God bless you!' This is not love on sight, Miss Fanny, for I have not yet seen you, but nevertheless I love you dearly, and I would proudly and fondly give you the homage and protection of a heart that has never sported with a woman's love. You will write me, Miss Fanny, I know you will write me candidly, frankly. I shall live trembling with uncertain but delightful hopes until I receive your letter; for although your heart may have already twined around some one of whom I have not heard—some manly soldier, some treasure of your heart, yet I will not believe it. It surely cannot be, that after suffering the perils and escapes of many battles, after the loss of my country's liberty, after all that is worth living for, *except love*, is gone, that I have survived the wreck to feel my own heart shattered with disappointment. I will not believe it yet. Write to me, dear Fanny, write to me, for I am now nothing but Cupid's culprit, convicted, condemned, and none but you can lift me up. Write to me, dear lady, and if you have regard for your patient, do let him see you—your shadow, your photograph. I know you would not be cruel because he was blind. He could not see the substance then—do not refuse him the shadow now. In any event, I shall expect that much.

" A hundred times' love for your mother, and ten thousand for yourself. I cannot write more now, for my new eyes are aching. When you reply, tell me every thing, your joys, your sorrows, your past history. An autobiography in outline is what I want.

" Yours, forever, I hope.

" What do you think of that, George, coming from a soldier, a veteran who has marched up to batteries and bullets, who has looked death in the face and never winked an eye? What do you think of that?"

"Weakness, amazing weakness, Colonel, but what made her return it? Did you lose her and live?"

"Lose her, George! Lose her! Why, don't you know nothing; have you not heard? Let me read you her reply, and you can guess the balance. But, George, my friend, my old companion in arms, all this is confidential—it's sacred—I will trust you on the honor of a soldier.

"Miss Fanny says:

"COL. B——: In answering your letter, I presume your desires to be expressed in good faith, and to emanate from a sincere and brave soldier. I do so honor the brave who have perilled their lives upon the field of battle, that no suspicion of hypocrisy or deceit finds rest in my bosom in relation to the writer of such a frank and manly letter, and therefore I make bold to lay aside my reluctance to comply with your request, and now send you a brief and true history of myself. Nature and Nature's God incline me to seek an alliance with a congenial spirit, and there is no bright prospect in the future that would make a single life a life of blessedness to me. Therefore a candid exchange of our sentiments may possibly result in a future and happy union; but should it result in nothing, I feel that my maiden modesty will not be violated or my confidence abused by him to whom I now trust the following few pages.

"Neither poetry nor romance form any part of my uneventful life. In most respects I am, and have been, as many other females who live and love and pass away without being known or heard of beyond the narrow limits of their humble neighborhood. I have thus lived a simple and natural life, saving that perhaps I have shed a few more tears of sadness than was my share, and sooner have dispersed them as often as I reflect how much I have to be thankful for that others I know have not.

"My father is long since dead. He sleeps well where we have laid him by the cedar-tree in the garden; for we chose to bury him where careless voices would not disturb his rest, nor careless hands pluck the flowers from his grave. My grandfather was wealthy and extravagant. From many incidents and accidents which make up life, his wealth took wings and flew away, but not until I had acquired a fair and liberal education. Since the decay of his prosperity our misfortunes have come thick and fast. Passing years have worked many changes of condition, and even the overseer of my grandfather's slaves has so greatly prospered as now to boast of his plantations, and his pretty daughters with whom I gayly frolicked in the shady grove now honor me with a distant bow. Not for envy do I mention such things as these, for they are not heartless girls, and would freely help me were I in actual want. They only feel the distance that wealth sometimes creates. They move in a different sphere, and have many, many things and fashionable cares to absorb their attention and beget an indifference to poverty.

"Such changes, I have often thought, are the parents of

philosophy and reflection, and therefore prove eminently useful to society and virtue. If we look at life by generations, it is but the see-saw that children play, and there is scarcely a family in our land who cannot illustrate, in either its ancestry or itself, the ups and downs, the grandeur and humility, the wealth and poverty that time is ever alternating. Therefore, I am neither covetous nor touched with envy, though very humble is my lot; for it may change before I die. Indeed, I know it will, if this our correspondence should ever make me the wife of a manly youth who would take me as his Genevieve, his bright and trusting bride. No lay of Eastern minstrels, no tender song of gentle sorrow, will he have to sing to win me, for my own sad song is sad enough to move me to the shelter of his manly bosom.

"Before this unhappy war, I had a brother so dear and kind that, had he lived, would have told me how I should write, and what I should say in this unmaidenly letter, for he would have loved and protected me all through the bright and the weary days of my life. His manly form has been for many months mouldering in a soldier's shallow grave, and the same brave troops fought over him at the second battle of Manassas that fought with him at the first. Oh, how we loved him, and how we love him yet! The night after he fell I dreamed I heard him call, and saw him beckon to me from out the spirit-land. My dream was like a prophet's vison, and the sad news, when it came, only confirmed my trembling fears. Since that dark hour, I have loved to sing :

'Call on, dear Will; no sound of lute or lyre—
No prayer of minister, or tale of heavenly joys,
No rich reward to which the good aspire,
Can call me heavenward like thy gentle voice.

'Then call me oft, nor let the year go round
Without a daily beckon from thine angel hand;
A sister's memory still loves the sound
That bids her join thee in the spirit-land.'

"My dear mother and I now live alone, all alone; and when I think that passing years will soon alas! too soon remove her from me, and that before many more seasons shall come and go, I shall be like a lonely leaf, trembling upon its stem, a fawn of the forest whose dam will never return, I feel sad and sorrowful, and involuntarily sing the sweet and plaintive ballad of 'Blue-eyed Mary.' At such times I have wished to twine like a helpless vine around some brave, good heart, some ideal of my wandering fancy, some real personation of my dreams, who would not hereafter blame me for imagining that I love him now. And could I not love him, and would I not, and shall not my heart feel glad, that one from whom I had no expectations, and whose sealed eyes had never looked into my own, should remember me with such earnest expression of his love, and must I conceal from him the kindling hopes which burn and glow as I think of the dark and lonely future?

"One day when you asked me of my brother, and placed your hand upon mine, I felt in my heart that your friendship and my sympathy was sincere, and that you were sad because of my grief. Even then, I had a shadowy hope that you might love me, but it soon vanished, and I thought no more of it until you said good-bye. You then revived my lingering suspicions, and since your departure, I confess to have thought of you often, very often, and waited for something, I know not what. Love, at sight, is not a weakness of my nature, but many a time, while you were our patient, I felt that it would be an easy thing for me to love you *if I dared.* But I steeled my heart against false hopes, and so you must not be surprised that I be easily won.

"But what shall I tell you of myself, and can I write the truth without suspicion of self-praise? and should I write less, I would not be truly answering the inquiries of your letter.

"One more year, and the spring flowers will have bloomed a score of times since I was christened as Fanny May. Until my fourteenth year, I lived and laughed as other merry girls who know no want and are driven to no necessity. With them I built my play-houses, and decked them with the broken china, climbed the low wood-shed, swung from the drooping branches of the trees, made pyramids in the sand, and picked berries on the road to school. Evenly and quietly I moved along in my studies, and thanks to a faithful teacher, and to a mother ever watchful, I acquired a love of study, and a taste for reading the choice library which was retained from the wreck of my father's fortune. When brought to the sad reality of our loss, I cheerfully began my household duties, and still continue as the maid of domestic work. No branch of such employment is now unknown to me, nor unwelcome to be performed for those I love. Sometimes we have a visitor, and then it does not take me long to make my toilet and receive the honored guest, for unlike the fair children of wealth, I do not have to study long the lights and shadows of many robes before I decide what apparel will best suit the company and the occasion. My father has often told me that men were the better judges of what a woman's manners should be to plese *his* sex, and taught me to be ever natural in my conduct and conversation, and never disguise the truth. So I do not feel mortified when seen carrying water from the spring, or planting the garden, or trimming the cedar hedge. Our wants are few, for it takes but little to support two lonely and humble females who cannot aspire to imitate the great. Until my brother's death, the profits from a small amount of bank stock were sufficient for our support, and the proceeds of his labor brought us many comforts, which now we cannot afford. But sufficient unto the day is the evil thereof, and we have never suffered or feared, nor will the promise made to the widow and the orphan be forgotten or unfulfilled.

"Thus much have I written as the outline of my life. My aspirations have been few, but my hopes are strong and earnest. An ever-welcome friend has proposed to secure me a situation as a teacher in a neighboring village, but it is too far for a daily walk, and I cannot bear to be separated from my home and mother, and my father's much-loved grave; and now, as I write to you, and try to feel altogether unselfish, and dream of happiness to come, and ever-living faith in him to whom I could trust my honor and my life, I am compelled to say that he who chooses me must choose my dear fond mother with me, during her pilgrimage on earth. No other condition do I impose, no other boon shall I presume to ask.

"You ask me for my photograph; I am sorry I have none. I have a miniature, but it is not like me now. I will send you my shadow so soon as it can be procured, and until then, for your edification, I will describe myself to you as a substitute for the picture. But I do not know that I ought to send you any thing, for it occurs to me that if you are so ardently in love, you will soon, very soon come here and claim the substance. After you have seen me, you would not need a photograph, for if I pleased you, would you not have a shadow on the brain? But to begin, excuse me for saying that my mother thinks me fair, and my fond brother often called me good and pretty. I am not an angel nor a peri of a poet's paradise; but who does not wish to be beautiful and to be thought so by the world, and is it wrong to feel such innocent ambition? The mirror that flatters our features is ever the most highly prized, and it is a universal pleasure to receive the delicate flattery of our friends. How well do I remember with what trembling inquiry I once asked my ever-candid mother if I was really beautiful, as my fond brother said, when he would stroke my hair, and press my cheek to his? How surprised she seemed, and started, for fear I was nursing vanity, and how tenderly reproachful was her voice when she replied, 'Fanny, you look well enough, but you are not beautiful. You are not grown, nor your form and features rounded as they will be, but you will be beautiful if you are good.'

"Now I am grown and in the bloom of perfect health; still I can pass along and dazzle no one, nor rob one soul of rest, nor scarce attract a moment's gaze of those I meet. With humble and unattractive dress I cheerfully perform my duties, and no 'valenciennes,' nor 'point,' nor 'honiton,' nor flounce, nor frill, nor sweeping trail, nor glittering jewels assist the eye to see the charms, *if any*, that I have. Sometimes I am vain enough to think that should the blessing of wealth be added to my lot, some of those who know me now might wonder that the flower of the forest could bloom so fair for being transplanted to a richer soil.

"But I cannot be so vainly personal. Let me finish by using the third person, and say I know a lady whose complexion once was fair but now has that shade of brunette which constant exercise has delicately painted there, almost hiding the blue veins of her temples. Her hair is dark, her eyes are hazel, secreting behind them full chalices of tears that well up to the surface too often and too easy, but then there are many smiles lurking near which are quick, very quick, to come forth and chase the tears back to their hidden fountains. Her voice has something of melody and tune, though she is no nightingale, and her form something of symmetry, though no model for an Italian sculptor. Her features are neither remarkable nor peculiar, but form a face of some expression, rather pleasant than otherwise, and might improve by reflection from the looks of one who would love her and listen while she sang 'Am I not fondly thine own?' This lady cannot enrapture any one with sweet and swelling notes upon the harp or the piano, for the lessons that she easily learned have faded from her memory. She cannot dance, though her steps are quick and free. Indeed, there are many things she cannot do that others might, but for all such womanly defects she can the better love, honor, and obey a true and noble man.

"This is all, dear sir, and enough, I fear, to make you doubt my maiden modesty. I feel already that I ought not to have written it, but still my pen has followed my thoughts, and my thoughts were provoked by a desire to please you, you, only you.

"My mother sends her love, and both of us our thankful rejoicings that you have been fully restored to light and life.

"I am yours forever, if—if—if—it is my destiny.

"FANNY."

"What do you think of that, George? Do you aspire to ever be happy enough to get such a letter?"

"I do not," said I; "but bachelor as I am, and until now casemated against the charms of the sex, I would have married that girl. Where is she, Colonel?"

The rustling of dressess announced the approach of females through the hall. They had returned the back way and the Colonel met them at the door of the veranda, and, with face all glowing with delight, introduced me to his wife as Fanny May. I don't know that I ever was more confused in my life, for I had not dreamed of his marriage, and was thinking of Miss Fanny as far away. She was a queen, and had I not fallen in love with the Colonel's sister, I can't say how long our friendship would have been unbroken. The Colonel is now my brother-in-law, and I declare myself to be as happy and proud as himself, and I did not have occasion to copy his love-letter.

AN ENIGMA.

(NOT PRAED'S.)

HIGH on the Alabama's deck, and ever full in sight,
My 1st is always present, and the last to leave the fight.
My 2d is a man of ease, upon whose pillowed breast
The wounded soldier loves to lean, the fainting man to
rest.
My 3d—the kind of honors, which, though worthy of our
aim,
Have never yet been reached or won by Semmes of naval
fame.
Nor can his foes impute to him the sin that makes my
4th,
A sin that bears the scorn and hate of all the brave of
earth.
My 5th, more kind and Christian, of peace and love did
write,
And to her moral fictions attention did invite.

My 6th gives caste and dignity unto the Irish name,
And marks the patriot for his wealth, his family, or his fame.
Unchanged, and still infallible, ere since the world begun,
Old Time has never moved my 7th, though he has moved the sun.
My 8th—the earliest bugle-note that leads the charger on,
That calls up Reynard from his rest, and wakes the trembling fawn.
Facing the east at early dawn, the crescent subject prays;
Unto my 9th ejaculates, and sings Mahomet's lays.
My last, the kind of pension, to every traitor due;
May this reward, in our day, be merited by few.
Now all the words above defined, some hidden and some plain,
Reversed and forwards, still they do in letters spell the same.
Take the 1st letter from each word, and place them side by side,
You have *my whole*—a statesman's boast—a mighty monarch's pride.

* * * * * * * * *

Three times an English chevalier, with bold and fearless breast,
Threw down his knightly gage, and dared the Turks unto the test,

He slew them one by one, and then he bore his prize away,
And thence he sought a distant land, where pilgrims went to pray.
But when misfortune came, and he laid trembling near his grave,
My whole, though weak and powerless, resolved his life to save:
The bold resolve was fortunate, success the effort crowned,
And "*Windsor Shades*" unto this day is known as classic ground.

THE END.

PROSPECTUS

OF THE

METROPOLITAN RECORD,

AND NEW YORK VINDICATOR.

ENLARGEMENT OF THE PAPER

FROM SIXTY-FOUR TO EIGHTY COLUMNS.

THE POLITICAL PLATFORM OF THE RECORD.

After the publication of the 26th number of the RECORD, of last year, we increased ITS SIZE from SIXTY-FOUR to EIGHTY COLUMNS. IT IS NOW THE LARGEST DEMOCRATIC AND FAMILY PAPER PUBLISHED IN THE UNITED STATES; and, although our expenses are very heavily increased by the change, we supply the paper AT THE SAME PRICE. The reading matter is of a more varied and interesting character, on account of the greater space placed at our disposal, and which is equal to FOUR ADDITIONAL PAGES, or SIXTEEN COLUMNS. We are encouraged to this change by the success that has attended our efforts to present the public with a paper that has held fast, through every vicissitude, to the two cardinal principles of State Rights and Self-Government, and that refused amid the fearful conflict of the past four years to lower the banner on which those principles were inscribed. We feel certain that this effort on our part to render our paper in every way deserving of the continued support of our friends, will be met by a generous and active coöperation on theirs in enabling us to extend its circulation. We know it will gratify them to be told that, despite the malice and persecution of our political enemies, despite the suppression of the RECORD and the arrest of its editor, despite the official power which was wielded to our disadvantage and material injury, we have been enabled to weather the storm in which so many went down, and are now looking forward with hope to a greater degree of usefulness in the future. For our part, we have no change whatever to make in our principles. The great political dogmas enunciated by the men of 1776, are as true to-day as they were then; and, though they have been forgotten by the people and trampled under foot by arbitrary power, it is only by a return to them that popular freedom can be saved from the dangers by which it is beset, through fanatics on the one hand, and designing and unprincipled politicians on the other.

We see no reason, after a full survey of the whole political field, to despair of the ultimate success of the principles for which we have contended. Force has been applied, and it has not decided, because it was not competent to decide, that the principles of State Rights and Self-Government have ceased to exist. It is needless to pursue this subject further, as its force must be apparent to every unbiased and impartial mind.

The future is before us, and as a journalist we shall perform our duty hereafter as we have performed it in the past. We have, as we said, no change to make. The RECORD'S platform of principles remains the same. It will be henceforward its aim to be a truthful and unswerving exponent of State Rights, and it is therefore inflexibly opposed to the anti-Democratic policy of consolidation. Believing that popular freedom in this Republic is dependent upon State Sovereignty, it is at war with all despotic encroachments on that principle and the rights of the people. It shall never cease to advocate the supremacy of the Civil Authority, and to denounce and condemn the pretensions and usurpations of Military Power.

In the future, as in the past, the RECORD will continue the faithful advocate of Democratic principles. It is true that recent events, brought about by a fanatical interference with the rights of States, and by an intolerance of the Constitution and laws made in accordance therewith, have caused a temporary revulsion; but the principles of the great revolution are only kept in abeyance, and will, we believe, be reasserted ere many years elapse. The people have yet to learn from experience that the lessons and teachings of the great statesmen who formed the Republic cannot be set aside unless by the total overthrow of popular freedom and self-government. No fact was more completely established, no principle more thoroughly vindicated, than that which asserts that "Government derives its just powers from the consent of the governed," and that a Union which can only be perpetuated by the strong arm of military power, must, if continued to be so sustained, result in the establishment of a centralized despotism.

The RECORD and VINDICATOR shall continue, as it has begun, the outspoken and fearless opponent of every act of unconstitutional policy, the defender of the great Charter of American Freedom, and the unflinching advocate of Liberty of Speech, Vote by Ballot, Habeas Corpus, Trial by Jury, Freedom of the Press, and State Rights.

LITERARY DEPARTMENT.

We devote special attention to this part of the RECORD, as each number bears ample testimony, and the "Portfolio" is one of its best and most successful features, blending, as it does, the humorous and the poetical with light sketches, anecdotes, and incidents in endless variety. All the contributions to this department are original, and the general approbation with which it has been received by the reading public stamps it as a complete success. We may add that the original poetry, which appears in this and other parts of the paper, is not surpassed, if it is equalled, by any journal, American or European.

THE FICTIONAL DEPARTMENT.

While ignoring the unhealthy and sensational style of too many of the current periodicals, we aim to make this department unsurpassed in point of interest to the best works of imagination, and shall leave nothing undone to render it equal, in its collection of original stories and tales, to the most popular and highest class of the fictional productions of the day. We are determined that no paper shall excel ours in this important feature, and that the younger portion of our patrons will find in its entertaining and pleasant reading a happy substitute for the dubious kind with which the country is unfortunately flooded.

THE EDITORIAL DEPARTMENT.

In our political platform we have presented the principles of the RECORD, and it shall be hereafter, as it has been in the past, our great object to sustain its reputation in this great and vital particular. The frank and outspoken manner with which all the subjects that properly come within the scope of this department have been treated, will be adhered to throughout. The editor firmly believes that the principles which he advocated and sustained during the late fierce and bloody four years' war, are, if possible, more essential now than ever, and that in their success alone can the great Revolution of '76 find its best and most practical development.

THE NEWS DEPARTMENT.

It is our aim to give in the Record a complete resumé of news, both through the correspondence and the general intelligence, prepared expressly for its columns. Our Foreign and Domestic Summary, in which the important intelligence of the day is given, is all rewritten, so that our readers are saved the trouble of poring over long and tedious statements and accounts to get at the points of the news. The commendation which this department of the Record has generally received is the best proof of its success.

MISCELLANEOUS.

In addition to the departments enumerated, we give from time to time art and scientific matters due attention, and occasionally present an interesting and instructive *melange* of miscellaneous reading.

The Metropolitan Record and Vindicator will be supplied to Subscribers on the following terms:

To City Subscribers, served by carriers.....$5 00 per year.
To Country Subscribers, served by mail.... 4 00 "
To Clubs of ten or more................. 3 00 "

(payable in advance).

Terms to Advertisers:

Special Notices........................25 cts. per line.
To Transient Advertisers...............15 "
To Yearly Advertisers..................10 "

All orders and communications should be addressed to the editor, No 424 Broome Street.

☞ The Editor would ask as a favor that his Subscribers would furnish him with the names and addresses of their friends in other States, as well as that in which they reside, that he may have the opportunity of supplying them with specimen copies of the Record, which he will do without any cost to them.

www.ingramcontent.com/pod-product-compliance
Lightning Source LLC
LaVergne TN
LVHW050517100826
845148LV00002B/368